© KP's Publications.
Published in November 2005 by KP's Publications, Canberra
PO Box 402, Gungahlin, Australian Capital Territory 2912 Australia.
ABN 12 603 152 161
E-mail: info@kpspublications.com
Web: www.kpspublications.com

Attribution : Artist Daphne Wallace Gamilaroi/Ullaroi language groups.
Cover title – Gamilaroi & Ullaroi Symbols ©
Editing: Russell Lane
Layout: Geoff Ross
Cover design: Pankaj Goel
Print production: PASS Global Pty. Ltd. T/A E Impressions

National Library of Australia
Cataloguing-in-Publication entry:
Sharma, Kamlesh.
Indigenous Governance.
Bibliography.

ISBN 0 9758028 0 1.
1. Business enterprises, Aboriginal Australian.
2. Councils, Aboriginal Australian.
3. Torres Strait Islanders - Societies, etc.
4. Corporate governance -Australia. I. Title. 305.89915

This work is copyright. Apart from any use permitted under the *Copyright Act* 1968, no part may be reproduced without the written permission of Dr Kamlesh Sharma of the publisher, KP's Publications.

Part of the proceeds from the sale of this book will be used for:
- Incentives to encourage Aboriginal and Torres Strait Islander students to enter tertiary education in Australia (to be managed by Aboriginal Hostels Limited); and
- Support for students of poor background to enter tertiary education in the Fiji Islands (to be managed by the University of Fiji).

Forthcoming books from the author:
Rahul's Road: *Reflections of a Fijiindian* (July 2006) ISBN 0 9758028-1-X.
Life Experiences of a Indo-Fijian: *The Challenges* (December 2006) ISBN 0 9758028-2-8

To all Indigenous organisations

INDIGENOUS GOVERNANCE

Dr Kamlesh Sharma

PUBLICATIONS
ACT 2912 Australia

INDIGENOUS GOVERNANCE

Dr Kamlesh Sharma

CONTENTS

Foreword
Preface
Acknowledgement

Chapter 1:	**Introduction**	 17

  Background
  Study problem and questions
  Study problem
  Theoretical framework

Chapter 2:	**Corporate Governance Background**	 21

  Introduction
  What is corporate governance?
  Corporate governance - differences in viewpoints
  Roles of the board and management
  Defining the board's role
  Defining the chairperson's role
  The role of the board v the role of the management
  Theoretical framework
  Agency theory
  Stewardship theory
  Agency theory v stewardship theory

Chapter 3:	**Indigenous Governance**	 33

  History of first Australians
  Aboriginal and Torres Strait Islander incorporated
     organisations
  Cultural theory
  Good corporate governance in non-profit sector
  Profit corporate governance principles in non-profit sector
  Gaps in study
  Study problem
  Study questions
  Background to the model of corporate governance
  Board skills
  Board appointments
  Board induction and training
  Board independence

Code of conduct
Strategy setting
Financial and operational reporting
Monitoring the performance of the board
Committee structure

Chapter 4: **Indigenous Organisation's Perspective** 49
Population and sample size
Location of the sampled organisations
Ethical considerations
Responses received from the sampled organisations
Geographical spread of the responses received
Patterns of data for study questions
What it means for the corporate governance model
Board skills
Board appointments
Board induction and training
Board independence
Board meetings and resources
Code of conduct
Strategy setting
Financial and operational reporting
Monitoring the performance of the board
Committee structure

Chapter 5: **Conclusions and Recommendations** 59
Conclusions about study questions
Conclusions about the corporate governance model
Corporate governance model: study findings
Corporate governance checklist for urban and sub-urban
    Indigenous organisations
Corporate governance checklist for rural and remote
    Indigenous organisations
Implications for theory
Implications for policy and practice
Limitations
Further study
Final remarks

Bibliography 73
Author's Profile
Commendations

FOREWORD

This is a pioneering work on Indigenous Governance.

Corporate governance in Indigenous organisations is an important issue that interests many different groups not only in Australia but around the world. This book, about Indigenous governance and, in particular, within the Aboriginal and Torres Strait Islander organisations, reveals that the corporate governance concepts have been mainly built around western theories. We urgently need more research in the Indigenous governance area to ascertain its suitability in the contemporary cultural context. I am presently involved in a study at the Australian National University. It is hoped the outcomes of this study will build on the work outlined in this book.

There have been studies in the non-profit sector to ascertain if a template for a governance structure from the profit sector would fit into any non-profit sector organisations, the outcome has been that no one formula fits all situations and that every non-profit sector organisation is unique: it has to customise the governance structure to its particular circumstances. This is equally true for Indigenous governance.

It is fair to say that most of the books in the corporate governance field focus mainly on profit sector. This book is different because it examines Indigenous governance in Australia.

I do not intend to summarise the book, however I would like to highlight some of the points that I think are important. The book explicitly illustrates that the use of corporate governance principles would increase participation and effectiveness in Aboriginal and Torres Strait Islander incorporated organisations. It reviews the various concepts of corporate governance and postulates the development of the cultural theory that is empirically tested during the survey of the selected organisations.

Briefly, some of the major findings of the book are that the various conditions attached by funding bodies rarely consider cultural issues facing Indigenous organisations. Indigenous people would participate more in the organisations' activities if these bodies considered cultural aspects in any corporate governance requirements.

Rarely is there any evaluation of training, pre-assessment of training, post-assessment of training and on-going knowledge assessment of directors to maintain currency of the knowledge and expertise required in fulfilling the role and responsibilities of a director. This work clearly shows that there is need for a separate corporate governance checklist for the urban and sub-urban Indigenous organisations. The needs and aspirations of

Indigenous peoples are as diverse as they are complex and no one size fits all approach will alone satisfy the specific requirements for governance of Indigenous peoples wherever they live.

This book provides a solid foundation for further study that will be imperative in order to obtain a deeper understanding of the issues involved.

Finally, this book offers guidance on Indigenous governance not only in Australia but elsewhere as well, where corporate governance practices are of increasing and immense importance. I am delighted to be able to recommend this pioneering book on Indigenous governance.

Professor Mick Dodson AM
Director, National Centre for Indigenous Studies
Australian National University
Canberra, November 2005

PREFACE

This book is based on the thesis completed in February 2003 for Doctoral studies in Business Administration through the Southern Cross University in Lismore, NSW. The title of the thesis was: 'Scope for the application of corporate governance concepts in the management of the Aboriginal and Torres Strait Islander incorporated organisations in Australia.' A concerted effort has been made to include materials in this book in a less formal academic way. Those readers who are interested in a more academic version of the analysis are encouraged to refer to the actual thesis. The thesis has been made available to the following Institutions and is available to interested readers and researchers subject to the guidelines and rules of the respective libraries:

- Australian Institute of Aboriginal and Torres Strait Islander Studies, Acton, Canberra, Australian Capital Territory.
- Australian National University, Canberra, Australian Capital Territory.
- Charles Darwin University, Darwin, Northern Territory.
- Curtin University, Perth, Western Australia.
- James Cook University, Townsville, Queensland.
- National Library of Australia, Canberra, Australian Capital Territory.
- Southern Cross University, Lismore, New South Wales.
- University of Ballarat, Victoria.
- University of British Columbia, Vancouver, Canada.
- University of Canberra, Australian Capital Territory.
- University of New England, Armidale, New South Wales.
- University of South Australia, Adelaide, South Australia.
- University of Technology, Sydney, New South Wales.

An electronic copy of the thesis is also available online at http://wwwlib.umi.com/dissertations/preview/3096577. The on-line publication reference number is AAT 3096577.

Enjoy and happy reading!

ACKNOWLEDGEMENT

I acknowledge the generous support of friends, colleagues and family who all gave their time, expertise and reassuring encouragement. I thank all those individuals who urged me to publish my work on Indigenous Governance; their efforts have finally paid off with the publication of this book. I am also very thankful to Professor Mick Dodson AM of the Australian National University for agreeing to write a foreword for the book. My sincere gratitude goes to Professor Satendra Pratap Nandan of the University of Canberra who provided encouragement, advice and guidance throughout this publishing project.

Special mention and appreciation goes to my colleagues, Mr Russell Lane for the editing, Mr Geoff Ross for the layout of the book and Mr Pankaj Goel for his selfless hours spent on the design. I am very appreciative of the artist Daphne Wallace for allowing me to use her art for this book.

Finally, this book is the result of countless hours of commitment, continuous encouragement, and patience of my family especially the dedication of my wife Amina, my children Rajnesh, Kamini, Komal & Priya, daughter-in-law, Ranjeeta and grandson, Rahul. It was only through their understanding and sacrifice that I have been able to complete this challenging project.

Dr Kamlesh Prasad Sharma
Canberra, November 2005

CHAPTER 1

INTRODUCTION

Background

This book arose from research into how the use of corporate governance principles could increase participation and effectiveness in Aboriginal and Torres Strait Islander incorporated organisations.

The term corporate governance has been given a wide range of meanings. These range from narrow definition which focuses on the processes by which a board of directors (the board) is accountable to the organisation's owners to the broad definition which focuses on the processes by which the board is accountable to all stakeholders, including owners, creditors, employees and the community.

The various definitions of the term corporate governance is well summarised as being concerned with the process by which corporate bodies are subjected to accountability mechanisms.

Previous researchers have tried to reconcile the difference between the western values and the Indigenous values but this has not been done in a wider context. There's also been study in the non-profit sector to ascertain if a template for a governance structure from the profit sector would fit into any non-profit sector organisations. The outcomes of these studies have been that one size does not fit all and that every non-profit sector organisation is unique. Each non-profit sector organisation has to customise the governance structure to its particular circumstances.

There is no doubt a gap in the study in terms of the applicable corporate governance structures for Aboriginal and Torres Strait Islander incorporated organisations in Australia. This is an area that needs to be explored to ascertain the scope for the application of the corporate governance principles in the management of these organisations in Australia.

Study problem and questions

This study builds a framework within which Aboriginal and Torres Strait Islander incorporated organisations can adopt and customise the model of corporate governance to their individual requirements.

Study problem

The central study problem is: 'What is the scope for the application of corporate governance concepts in the management of the Aboriginal and Torres Strait Islander incorporated organisations in Australia.'

The problem addressed in this study is: 'How can the use of corporate governance principles increase participation and effectiveness in Aboriginal and Torres Strait Islander incorporated organisations.'

Essentially, a template model of corporate governance cannot be applied to the Aboriginal and Torres Strait Islander incorporated organisations. The model will need to be customised to fit into the individual needs of the organisations.

Theoretical framework

The theories relevant to corporate governance are the agency theory, stewardship theory, and the cultural theory that provide a theoretical background to this study.

The agency theory approach holds that managers will not act to maximise the returns to shareholders unless appropriate governance structures are implemented to safeguard the interests of shareholders. The agency theory sees companies as a nexus of contracts where differences between the interests of stakeholders must be minimised amongst other things by corporate governance practices.

The stewardship theory assumes that managers are principally motivated by achievement and responsibility needs and given the needs of managers for responsible, self-directed work, organisations may be better served to free managers from subservience to non executive director dominated boards. In the stewardship model, managers are good stewards of the corporations and diligently work to attain high levels of corporate profit and shareholders returns.

The cultural theory of corporate governance illustrates the difference in the perceptions from the dominant western society and its values and the Aboriginal people. Conceptualisation of culture based on a mainstream structural functionalist perspective fails to examine how culture is embedded and entangled in the exercise of power, resistance, and conflict in a given society.

The importance placed on sharing and relatedness in Indigenous enterprises illustrates the difficulty of applying western-based management theories in this context. A major reason for the failure of many intervention programs is that they do not recognise the validity and effectiveness of existing social and organisational structures.

In summary, this study made four contributions. Firstly, the study findings will enable the Indigenous communities to apply the recommendations to their respective organisations in order improve and strengthened their corporate governance practices. Secondly, it will guide funding bodies to consider cultural issues facing Indigenous organisations to ensure success of its programs. Thirdly, the study will enable Indigenous communities to handle the training requirements of its directors more effectively. Finally, the study laid the foundation for other researchers who choose to examine the corporate governance issues in Indigenous organisations.

CHAPTER 2

CORPORATE GOVERNANCE BACKGROUND

Corporate governance principles and concepts became the centre of attention for organisations in the late 1980's following some major collapses of corporations around the world. This led to a change of attitude with a much higher expectation being placed on officers of corporations to perform. These expectations applied equally to profit and non-profit organisations.

Introduction

The starting point for any discussion on corporate governance is the creation of the registered company. The registration of the company dates back to the *Joint Stock Companies Act* 1844 (UK), although there is some evidence that a broader concept of corporate governance can be traced back to the Swiss cantons of the early 14th century. It was the development of registered companies that seemed to make the difference, in particular the passing of the *Limited Liability Act* 1855 (UK) to protect shareholders from debt beyond their investment. The British influence in subsequent periods of history meant the basic company law and corporate governance principles were adopted throughout the Commonwealth, including Australia, Canada, Hong Kong, India, New Zealand, Singapore and South Africa.

Following the collapse of many corporate entities around the world in the late 1980's, the spotlight focused on the board rather than on management of the company. Managers run the business, but the board members and officers are to ensure it is being run effectively and in the right direction. Thus good managers do not necessarily make good directors, as they require a different skill set.

A successful director needs the ability to think strategically, communicate effectively and act decisively. The role calls for knowledge, experience and integrity, something that has been missing in corporate Australia recently. An example is the recent corporate collapses such as the HIH Insurance Group, One Tel Communications Limited and Ansett Airlines.

Non-profit organisations are as accountable as profit organisations. The literature reflects the need to ensure that corporate governance structures in a non-profit organisation are similar to profit organisations. The non-profit sector has not been immune from fluctuation in the broad macro-economic environment. Where fluctuations have been negative it has been incumbent on the non-profit organisations in all sectors to respond in a more efficient manner. Voluntary associations in general don't have a brilliant operational history.

Within non-profit organisations stakeholders do question policies and processes that may allow significant losses and low ethical and professional standards while under the traditional model of corporate governance, the board of directors manage the corporation and set business policy. Modern boards of directors have practically nothing to do with the day-to-day business of the corporation.

Before the board may undertake its duty the board as a whole must have goals and some basic rules that it uses in management of itself.

A board should agree on how it is to manage itself before the management of the company's affairs. This includes:
- its composition, its agenda process and performance;
- clear understanding of director's term of tenure and how new appointees are nominated and chosen;
- process to monitor the Chief Executive Officer (CEO);
- performance review measures of the board;
- process to review compensation plans, succession plans;
- processes to develop a strategic and business plans; and
- issues of internal control.

What is corporate governance?

The term corporate governance has been given a wide range of meanings. These range from narrow definition which focuses on the processes by which the board is accountable to the organisation's owners to the broad definition which focuses on the processes by which the board is accountable to all stakeholders, including owners, creditors, employees and the community.

Those using the term corporate governance will often choose the definition that most nearly approximates the spin, which they are seeking to develop. Equally those using the term will often make use of the fuzziness of the definition in order to incorporate a range of meanings into a particular discussion. It is therefore important to identify the way in which the term is used in any particular context.

The various definitions of corporate governance are well defined in general terms as being concerned with the process by which corporate bodies are subjected to accountability mechanisms. Corporate governance is the balancing of managerial risk taking, entrepreneurial energy and some form of monitoring, so that management's direction is aligned with the interests of those who have entrusted their capital to the enterprise and, to a lesser extent, the interests of other stakeholders.

Corporate governance is all of the influences affecting the institutional processes, including those for appointing the controllers and/or regulators, involved in organising the production and sale of goods and services. Described in this way, corporate governance includes all types of firms whether or not they are incorporated. The benefits of corporate governance as a board which has control over the strategy of the company, it is transparent and accountable and has well defined procedures, is likely to be a board which serves its shareholders well.

Generally the constitution should reflect an appropriate foundation for the enterprise to flourish. Therefore corporate governance includes how an organisation achieves its purpose. The essence of governance is found in the relationship between various participants in determining the direction and performance of the organisation. The primary groups involved in this relationship are the shareholders, the board of directors and the management. They also include customers, suppliers, creditors and the community.

As a result, corporate governance has a wider stakeholder base than just the board and members. It includes the underlying driver at the board level. The prevailing view of corporate governance holds that shareholders need more control or influence over managers to prevent managers providing lackluster performance in managing the enterprise. Corporate governance has become fixated on the relationship between management and shareholders but has ignored employees and advocates and the principle that directors of companies should represent all stakeholders, not just shareholders.

Corporate governance - differences in viewpoints

The reasons for the diverse views on the definition of corporate governance are simply due to the fact that it has been related to different cultural contexts, intellectual backgrounds and interests of writers.

However, some writers do not accept that publicly traded corporations should be responsive to the rights and wishes of stakeholders. Some believe that the stakeholder theory is both misguided and mistaken, and that stakeholder theory of accountability is unjustified, as it undermines private property, agency and wealth, is incompatible with business and with corporate governance.

The diversity of view about corporate governance is due to the lack of a broad defining paradigm, which has created a sense of intellectual vertigo in the debate over corporate governance reforms.

Workers in the field of corporate governance come from different academic disciplines. There is often little, or incomplete, integration between the various disciplines. The overlap of corporate governance with other disciplines is rarely articulated or recognised. To indicate how different viewpoints arise, and to provide an overview of this topic, an example is highlighted below.

The phrase corporate governance is often applied narrowly to questions about the structure and functioning of boards. This view is found amongst some business school writers and management consultants. It defines corporate governance as the structure whereby managers at the organisational apex are controlled through the board of directors, its associated structures, executive incentive, and other schemes of monitoring and bonding.

This definition is focused on the boardroom but extends the scope to include owners and others interested in the affairs of the company, including creditors, debt financiers, analysts, auditors and corporate regulators.

Roles of the board and management

Ultimately, the success of every enterprise depends on the calibre of its directors and the effectiveness of its board. Yet, around the world, there are some very different ideas on what the role of directors should be and how boards should be structured and run.

Any board of an organisation that wishes to add value to its business must consider how to differentiate between the board's role and that of the management. It needs to start with the definition of the board's role.

Defining the board's role

The values and principles adopted by a board and other ethical considerations arising out of the board's relationships with stakeholders will influence how a board defines its role. A board, which adopts an ethical approach to its role, will ensure that a corporate philosophy and ethos is developed, articulated and put into practice. Such a board will tend to:
- Pay full regard to all relationships when making decisions;
- Ensure that that the company is operated according to best practice;
- Insist that the company observes the sprit as well as the letter of the law; and
- Ensure that the policies and practices of the company reflect the corporate philosophy and ethos.

Generally, regulatory requirements influence boards in defining their role and appropriate corporate governance practices. Other influences on the board in defining its role include society and government's views of the role of the corporation in today's society as well as 'best practice' corporate governance systems. Various codes, guidelines, and studies have been undertaken in the area of corporate governance and these will influence how a board differentiates its role with that of management.

Corporate governance practices reflect the differentiation between the role of the board and the role of the management, with the board defining its role by reference to numerous social, economic, ethical and political concerns, including:
- The board's view on the role of the corporation (agency or stewardship theory);
- Ethical considerations relating to the various relationships of the company; and
- The legal context in which the board operates.

Six strategies that can be used to keep the board focused on the association priorities instead of being focused on the operational minutiae. The six strategies can be applied to all non-profit boards and these are to:
- ensure all directors understand the board's role;
- establish a rapport and shared vision with the CEO;
- assess the association's particular situation;
- develop an action plan;
- give board members relevant information; and
- keep agenda focused on the big picture.

The strategies apply to the board members as well as to the CEO of the associations. It is more focused on the CEO's as they are the ones who can sway the board's emphasis and priorities much better than anyone else. There are ten basic responsibilities of non-profit boards that cannot be overlooked due to its importance. These responsibilities are as follows:
- determine the organisation's vision and purposes;
- select the CEO;

- support the chief executive and assess his or her performance;
- ensure effective organisational planning;
- ensure adequate resources;
- manage resources effectively;
- determine, monitor and strengthen the organisation's programs and services;
- enhance the organisation's public standing;
- ensure legal and ethical integrity and maintain accountability; and
- recruit and orient new board members and assess board performance.

As boards of directors have basic collective responsibilities, board members are also entrusted with individual responsibilities as part of board membership.

The obligations of board service are considerable and they extend well beyond the basic expectations of attending meetings and participating in fund raising activities. All non-profit organisations must formulate a clear statement of individual board member responsibilities adapted to the organisation's needs and circumstances. This would help with the process of recruiting new board members by clarifying expectations before candidates accept nomination, and it can provide criteria by which the committee responsible for identifying and recruiting prospective nominees can review the performance of incumbents who are eligible for re-election or re-appointment.

The chemistry of interpersonal relationships at board level can be sensitive and sometimes volatile. This requires good interpersonal skill that supplements the other required skills for an effective director. All corporations need good leaders on the board of directors. All boards (either profit or non-profit) have a captain that navigates or steers the ship in the right direction. These individuals are known by many names some of which are 'chairman', 'chairperson' or 'president'. The most common term used in the Australian context is 'chairperson'.

Defining the chairperson's role

The precise role of the chairperson varies greatly between organisations. The role is also influenced by the size of the organisation, its complexity and ownership structure. More importantly, is the personalities around the board table that will have a major impact, not only to organisational structure and direction, but also influencing the climate of the organisation.

Some chairpersons act as the spokesperson for their organisation and take a major role in relations with government bodies. However, for all chairpersons there is a set of core functions, which have to be performed if the organisation is to run well. These roles are as shown in the following table.

Core Functions

1. To lead the board so that it operates effectively.
2. To encourage the fellow directors to give their best to the company.
3. Responsible for creating the mood of the board to ensure subjects are properly addressed and all differing views are actually heard.
4. Must be strong and fair while being dedicated to the welfare of the organisation as a whole.
5. Try to get directors to understand the distinction between board functions and management functions and to confine themselves to the former.
6. Facilitates meetings that are inclusive as well as efficient.
7. Ensure accurate minutes of the meeting are kept.
8. Act as the representative and spokesperson of the board.
9. Act as a link between the board and management and particularly between the board and the CEO.
10. Ensure that adequate preparations have been made to identify and prepare the CEO's successor.
11. Be diplomatic and able to serve as a mediator.

The chairperson is the link between the board and the stakeholders and has the ultimate responsibility for the organisation's governance. This role includes reporting annually the results of the organisation.

The role of the board v The role of the management

The key role of the board should be to ensure that corporate management is continuously and effectively striving for above-average performance, taking account of risk, such as the self-interest of the managers at the expense of the company. This is not to deny the board's additional role with respect to shareholder protection. This definition of the role of the board leads to the following views of the board's functions:

- The board's prime responsibility is setting performance goals and monitoring management's progress in achieving the goals;
- The board should require management to develop strategies, policies and proposals on major decisions, instead of itself taking a decisionmaking and initiating role; and
- Management is accountable to the board for formulating proposals for the board and ensuring these proposals are implemented in practice.

On the other hand, increasing laws, regulations, court judgments, standards of best practice and the influence of institutional shareholders have led many to focus on conformance as the primary responsibility of the board.

The standards of compliance and conformance that are required of companies have been raised and the demands on directors have become much greater.

The twin pressures to conform to higher standards and to improve performance have, to a large degree, coincided with increasing demands on boards of directors that they accept greater accountability and that they make their managers more accountable to them. The weight placed by a board on its responsibility to ensure above-average performance and its responsibility to ensure conformance with laws, regulations, and community expectations will influence the corporate governance practices adopted by it. In this new millennium, all boards are expected to be operating within the corporate governance dicta that have emerged both internationally and in Australia in response to some of the experiences in the 1980s.

A range of bodies, from both public and private sectors, have issued reporting and behavioural guidelines, and organisations such as the Australian Institute of Company Directors and Chartered Secretaries Australia have played a prominent role in reinforcing the standards and expectations of behaviour and performance from all directors and officers.

All good boards have members who challenge and confront issues. They devote time necessary for preparation and participation and bring with them a rich body of experience to assist management. Poorly functioning boards are fraught with conflicts, have members who fail to attend meetings and are ill prepared. They have an atmosphere of cronyism, and lack of independence. They are unwilling to challenge decisions and information. They fail to ask questions necessary to get to the heart of corporate issues.

Corporate failures usually result from a few well-intentional but flawed management decisions that are not challenged in an efficient, effective manner. This is because of subtle failures in the decision-making process, in how boards and managers make decisions and monitor corporate governance.

Many of the standard reference works on management and organisations fail to draw any distinction between the role of management and that of the board of directors. Yet there is a proposition that there is a fundamental difference and this directly relates to corporate governance. One could express this as the role of management to run the enterprise and the role of the board is to see that it is being run well and in the right direction.

Theoretical framework

The approach a board takes to the relationship between itself, management, shareholders and other stakeholders can also influence the approach taken to defining the role of the board and that of management. In this respect, it is important to consider the theories relevant to corporate governance. All agency theory, stewardship theory, and the cultural theory provide a theoretical background to this book.

Agency theory

Agency theory explains how to best organise relationships in which one party (the principal) determines the work, which another party (the agent) undertakes. Problems arise in corporations because agents (top management) are not willing to bear responsibility for their decisions unless they own a substantial amount of stock in the corporation. The agency theory approach holds that managers will not act to maximise the returns to shareholders unless appropriate governance structures are implemented to safeguard the interests of shareholders.

In summary, the idea of agency theory has only been applied to directors and boards in the 1980's. Inherently the theoretical view is that people are self-interested rather than altruistic and cannot be trusted to act in the best interests of others, but rather maximise their own utility. The agency theory presents the relationship between the directors and the shareholders as a contract. Thus, the directors, acting as agents of the shareholders will take decisions in their own interests and thus be subject to transaction costs for the checks and balances necessary to reduce non-compliance over enforcement costs.

Stewardship theory

The stewardship theory assumes that managers are principally motivated by achievement and responsibility needs and given the needs of managers for responsible, self-directed work, organisations may be better served to free managers from subservience to non executive director dominated boards. Managers are good stewards of the corporations and diligently work to attain high levels of corporate profit and shareholder returns. The theory argues that over time, senior executives tend to view the corporation as an extension of themselves.

In summary, the classical idea of corporate governance is that the directors, on behalf of the shareholders, hold the various assets of a company on a trust. The directors are automatically fiduciaries and owe an equitable duty not to have a conflict of interest or make a secret profit at the expense of the shareholders. The powers of the company are exercised by the directors, who are appointed by, and are accountable to, members at a general meeting. An independent auditor produces a report to members to show the company accounts are true and fair. The stewardship theory remains the theoretical foundation for much regulation and legislation.

Agency theory v stewardship theory

Many proponents of Agency and Stewardship theory see each theory contradicting the other. Some possibilities are that the studies did not separate out the effect of firms being in a regulated industry or possessing a dominant shareholder acting as a supervisory board or relationship investor.

The assumption of opportunism on which agency theory is based can become a self-fulling prophecy whereby opportunistic behaviour will increase with the sanctions and incentives.

Likewise, stewardship theory could also become a self-fulling. The inclination of individuals to act as stewards or self-seeking agents may be contingent upon the institutional context. If this is the case, both theories can be valid as indicated by empirical evidence.

Stewardship theory, like agency theory, would then be seen as sub-set of political and other broader models of corporate governance. The principle of stewardship as similar to agency theory in which the CEO act as agents who are morally obligated to perform in a manner that is in the best interests of shareholders.

However, whereas agency theory tends to focus exclusively on agent/owner relationships, stewardship implies a broader range of CEO responsibilities. Organisational stewardship is based on trust that can be described as the psychological contract that exists between two parties with regards to expectations about the relationship.

CHAPTER 3

INDIGENOUS GOVERNANCE

The immediate discipline for the study is the non-profit sector organisations that are defined as those that have not been established, and are not managed, to make a profit for an owner or for distribution to shareholders. The Aboriginal and Torres Strait Islander incorporated organisations that represent the study population form part of the non-profit sector family.

The history of first Australians need to be considered briefly in the context of Indigenous governance before considering the roles of the Aboriginal and Torres Strait Islander incorporated organisations.

History of the first Australians

Except for the last few decades, being Aboriginal has, since 1788 meant living under controls imposed by people of another race. The legislation and bureaucracies developed in every Australian colony and state for managing Aborigines were, above all, instruments for control. They determined where Aboriginal people could live and work, who could visit them, what their accommodation and diet would be, what they did with their money, how their children would be raised, and whom they could marry. Except for prisoners, Aboriginal people have been the most tightly controlled group in Australian history.

Being Aboriginal meant being written about. Aborigines have been the subject of more studies in more academic disciplines than almost any other Indigenous population in the world; and they have received more media attention than any of the one hundred and fifty immigrant groups making up the rest of Australia's population. What is written is usually for non-Aboriginal audiences; Aboriginal people have had little control over the study; the results are rarely communicated to them; and they have had little right of reply where they have been misrepresented.

The foundation of the colony rested upon the spurious legal construct of Terra Nullius, according to which no people had a right to land, which they did not cultivate. This sanctioned the rape of Aboriginal land and legalism thereafter was used to deny even the procedural equality to the Indigenous population. Economic forces and social sanctions combined to control the conduct of race relations.

The Indigenous peoples of Australia are the Aboriginal and Torres Strait Islander peoples, who have lived here continuously for some two thousand generations. Other Australians are all those peoples who arrived on Australian shores or were born here, since 1788. That amounts to some nine generations. The difference between two thousand and nine generations is obviously great, but it does not seem to be a point that registers or sits easily in the psyche of most non-Indigenous Australians.

Two hundred years ago, Europeans came to a country inhabited by peaceful people living in harmony with their environment, with an ancient system of law and a highly developed system of social justice. Prior to colonisation, Indigenous people of Australia controlled all aspects of their life and were able to exercise self determination. They were able to shape their very being by ensuring their psychological fulfilment in incorporating the cultural, social and emotional well being into their lives. However, as colonisation evolved, the culture became fragmented as the people were forced onto the fringes of European society. The invaders and conquerors developed institutions and practices for the support of their own survival as the dominant force in the particular domain and the implementation of the colonial power's objectives. The interests of the indigenous, or the invaded, are of little concern particularly during the early years of conquest.

Wherever we look, at the European colonisers of Africa last century, or Indonesia colonisers of East Timor or West Papua in recent decades, we can see that policies and practices are dominated by a central concern – to secure the region in the interests of the colonising power. And the British Australia was no different, except that they had embraced the absurdity of Terra Nullius, and in various ways attempted to make it a reality.

Despite negative racial attitudes and detrimental government policies, the early colonisers were by no means unilaterally successful in over-riding and erasing the original culture. Aboriginal people have survived the devastating impact of colonisation with disruption to their lives, traditions, spirit and courage. Since the first contact, there has been deliberate and systematic disempowerment of their lands. The non-Indigenous Australian population should be more aware of the way Aboriginal children were taken away from their families and put into missions.

Particularly dangerous is the widespread stereotyping of Aboriginal people and culture. The stereotypes have a long and changing history. After being depicted as noble savages in the eighteenth century and a doomed race in the nineteenth, we must now come to terms with the images of the late twentieth century as being the drunken brawler, the development-defeating land rights activist, the dole-dependent neglecter of children, the improvident and squalid fringe dweller.

The point about such images is that non-Aboriginals create and use them for their own purposes. For example, environmentalists now vaunt tradition orientated Aboriginal groups the 'original conservationist'; Marxists speak of them as 'proto-communists'; feminists allude to their 'sexual egalitarianism'. The danger with all such idealised images is that few Aboriginal groups exactly match the model. In its simplicity, the model is doubly dangerous: it obscures the diversity and complexity of Aboriginal socio-cultural systems, and it misrepresents and devalues the people who fail to resemble it. Furthermore, it provides justification to those who, for their own ends, are determined to intervene in Aboriginal affairs.

The law was used against Aboriginal people as a mode of social control in the latter half of the nineteenth century. No longer were they an economic threat; still less were they a political threat. They were, however, a moral threat to a society where 'peace, order and good government' were the hallmarks of an advanced, a civilised, and a white socio-political order.

The twentieth century law played a more active and positivist role as an intervener; it regulates and promotes social change based on recognition of elemental human rights, needs and aspirations and latterly also predicated on social and sexuality equality. Prior to 1967 the federal government lacked the constitutional power to legislate for Aboriginals as a race. It could do so in ancillary topics like social security benefits, but it did so in a way, which disadvantaged the Aboriginal recipient.

Unrestricted federal franchise was not conferred until 1962 and then was accompanied by measures not applicable to the white voter. The several states and territories constructed a legal edifice, which varied in dimension, depth and time. No fewer than sixty-seven separate definitions or references were devised by statute law to describe Aborigines. The laws prescribed their lives for them based on their colour, their appearance, or their presumed proportion of 'Aboriginality'.

Aboriginal and Torres Strait Islander incorporated organisations

Australian experience with governance bodies for Indigenous peoples has produced several interesting innovations. Traditionally, since colonisation, governance has been seen as a matter for Governments. Little attempt was made to understand Aboriginal authority structures and processes; indeed, attempts were made to eradicate such structures and processes.

There was a need in the 1970's for Aboriginal people to establish additional structures for the purposes of receiving and administering royalty-equivalent monies from mining and other developments on Aboriginal land. While the Indigenous Australians were and remain able to establish corporations and associations under generally applicable Commonwealth and State or Territory legislation, there was a need for a more user-friendly system that could produce culturally appropriate corporate entities. The outcome was the Commonwealth legislation in the form of the *Aboriginal Councils and Associations Act* 1976.

The legislation, however, provided only one model for the governance structure, which resulted in many Indigenous organisations opting for incorporation under other jurisdictions. From a law intended to suit the enormously diverse needs of Indigenous groups and communities across Australia, the approach taken was that 'one model (size) fits all'. Only one governance model 'suit' was made available and that was a legal straitjacket, which gave no room for local cultural variation in corporate structures and decision-making processes.

The initial idea of legal incorporation into associations made little impact to Aboriginal and Torres Strait Islanders, but gradually its benefits (and its difficulties) became evident with some Indigenous groups and those working with them. The difficulties of reconciling the European basis of these incorporated bodies and the traditional practices of Aboriginal society were acute and the early years of their development provided a record of confusion, dissension, trial and error, failures and new beginnings. The spread of the Aboriginal incorporated association is evidence that its adoption encouraged a greater degree of Aboriginal self-management. The Aboriginal and Torres Strait Islander incorporated organisations are part of the wider non-profit sector.

It is important to recognise at the outset that the term non-profit in relation to an organisation does not mean that it does not make or indeed strive to make a profit. The primary difference between profit and non-profit organisations is that those operating in the non-profit sector are typically prohibited by statute or their constituent documents from distributing any profits they make to their members. However, members do get benefits in other ways if the organisation makes a profit.

Aboriginal and Torres Strait Islander organisations represent a commitment of like-minded people to provide service to their community without seeking personal financial reward or profit. As a result of this form of group commitment in Australia, such organisations are sometimes called 'community organisations'. In rural Australia, Aboriginal people constitute the permanent long-term population, a large number of which derive from the relocation of Aboriginal people to church or government run settlements. The political domain of these communities has been changing rapidly over the last twenty years. Since the early 1970's, these community organisations have been subject to government policy changes directed at establishing local government structures, fostering an ideology of Aboriginal local autonomy and practices of local accountability.

While none of these institutions have precedents in the indigenous structures of Aboriginal Australia, there are important cultural principles in the organisation of the formerly independent Aboriginal societies, which are relevant for the present debates about self-determination and land rights. Kinship, communality and the Dreaming continue to influence Aboriginal people's understanding of and political approach to present-day events.

Aboriginal people do not share a single, simple structure for the management of their public affairs. Aside from the differing scale of social affairs, there is also significant regional variation. There are also significantly different political outcomes in different parts of the country. These differences are sometimes the result of the varying success of group or individual interests in their competing claims for resources and leadership.

Cultural theory

The cultural theory of corporate governance illustrates the difference in the perceptions from the dominant western society and its values and the Aboriginal people.

Once we realise the problems and difficulties with western theories, we begin to recognise that possibly these difficulties may be due to our own limited and contingent understanding that there are other cultures, other forms of social life which rely on other conceptions, we start to apprehend the possibilities between Aboriginal people and the dominant society.

One of the core components of Australian Indigenous people's worldview is the classificatory kinship system that shapes and orders behaviour. The whole community is classified into specific relationships with each member.

For example, the Pitjantjatjara people of Central Australia gave Europeans kinship terms so as to draw them into the network of reciprocal relationships and thereby bring predictability to their dealings with them.

The Yolngu of the Northern Territory are also known to assign positions within the domain of Yolngu kinship to non-Aboriginal people with whom they have more than superficial or brief contact. Thus for many Indigenous peoples, kin positions constitute the basic datum of social identity.

Kinship rules prescribe what must be done, and also what must not be done in relation to matters of marriage, food gathering, sharing of food and other goods, trading among communities and educational roles. It imposes on members of the community obligations as to gift giving. This obligation arises from the principle of reciprocity and is exemplified in the notion of sharing. Individuals are expected to share food in certain ways, show respect to certain people, marry within a section, perform a ritual, avoid speaking to certain people, instruct another person or paint particular designs because the pattern laid down in The Dreaming dictated that it should be done.

For Australian Indigenous peoples the core value is relatedness. It is this relatedness, which produces a society where cooperation is valued over competition and where competition among individuals is discouraged. When making contacts with others it is the maintenance of personal relationships rather than the accurate handling of quantities or the keeping of prior agreements that takes priority. The significance of the exchange lies in fulfilling the act of reciprocity. The complexity and the diversity of the kinship system is some large part attributable to the regulation of marriage by kinship, not only negatively via rules prohibiting marriage between certain kinds of kin, but also positively via rules that define certain kinds of inter-kin marriage as proper or orthodox. Many languages include several distinct, though structurally interrelated, systems of kin classification, each of which is socially specialised.

In traditional Aboriginal culture, value is attached to participation, not productivity. It is considered sufficient to join in and share with other members of the community, no measure is applied as to whether or not a member's contribution to the group is enough. The value therefore lies in having made some contribution, thereby maintaining essential relationships within the Indigenous community. The majority of Indigenous peoples either refuse assimilation into the 'whitefella' ways, or simply cannot adapt to the demands associated with the 'whitefella' notions of work, even though they are well aware of 'whitefella' notions that govern the use of cash, promote the work ethics and turn labour into a creature of the market.

Indigenous attitudes to employment can only be understood in the light of kinship relations, and the priority placed on maintaining and strengthening these relations. The existence of shared financial obligations within family networks enables family groups to prioritise social relations over financial matters. Employment does not have the same economic imperative as for non-Aboriginal people. Many Indigenous people place no importance on continual employment, and work is generally regarded as an economic necessity, rather than as part of a lifetime plan. The importance placed on sharing and relatedness in Indigenous enterprises illustrates the difficulty of applying western-based management theories in this context.

Indigenous organisations and communities have been increasingly submitted to accountability and compliance that are in direct conflict with the core Australian Indigenous values of sharing and relatedness.

Among non-Indigenous organisations, traditional Aboriginal values are usually perceived as an impediment to economic development and organisational effectiveness. Reluctance to compete, a different orientation toward time, an emphasis on consensus decision making, and putting family needs before business goals are characteristics that are difficult to reconcile with modern capitalism. A major reason for the failure of many intervention programs is that they do not recognise the validity and effectiveness of existing social and organisational structures.

Study on the link between cultural values and managerial approaches in Canada suggests that management practices must be flexible, adaptable, and less ethnocentric. The spiritual core value of First Nation Canadians values is a vision of wholeness, where all things are interconnected and interrelated. From this spiritual core stems a respect for all forms of life and a sense of trust, sharing, kindness, humility, and harmony in relationships with others. Ideally it generates behaviour that is egalitarian, noninterfering, nonmanipulative, cooperative, and highly respectful of others. Individual freedom and autonomy are highly valued, providing that the dignity of others and the well being of the group and community are preserved. These values conflict with the non-Native culture, with its linear, analytical approach to thinking and its respect for assertiveness, competitiveness, individual achievement and the ability to influence and manipulate others.

Compared with the national cultures of Canada and United States, First Americans and First Nation Canadians cultures can be considered to be much more collectivist in orientation. Collectivism is directly related to traditional Native ideals that focus on the survival of the small group.

A primary value of Aboriginal cultures is striving to bring about the greatest harmony and collective good while honouring the freedom and autonomy of oneself and others. Wealth acquired by individual pursuit is expected to be shared for the collective good.

This contrasts with the individualistic or market view of the employment contract as simply an economic transaction between the buyers and sellers of labour. In collectivist cultures, the organisation often becomes the family or in-group to which members have a strong affiliation and loyalty. Leaders and staff are expected to show strong feelings of obligation to the in-group.

Good corporate governance in non-profit sector

For a board to review its own effectiveness, the members have to want to do so and be serious about it. While such a review cannot guarantee business success, the outcome is very likely to be a more effective board that is more than likely to lead to success. There is a need to develop, and broadly disseminate, additional user-friendly governance resources and tools to meet the needs of busy board members and CEO's.

The keys to success are easy to articulate but the doors to good governance are difficult to unlock during the normal course of human interactions and organisational politics. It takes a strong commitment to open communications and a good deal of hard work.

From a corporate governance perspective, the private corporate form cannot simply be grafted into the corporatisation process because the government needs to retain the power of indirect persuasion which requires significant changes to the corporate form and the relationships that exist within the corporate form as between the shareholders, the company and the directors.

The retention of the power to direct and the requirement that directions be taken into account is so fundamental as to strip away any prospect that such bodies can apply principles of good corporate governance in the way that are applicable to listed companies.

Government regulation can restrict the implementation of good corporate governance principles and this can apply to the wider non-profit sector as well. This is possible as government has the power to make laws that could be seen to force the organisations to be managed in a particular way. This could be either restrictive or encouraging good governance but a lot depends on the nature of the legislation and the agenda of the government.

The Aboriginal and Torres Strait Islander communities are at the mercy of funding bodies and the plethora of departments and agencies all vying for their programs to be delivered within their guidelines, which in most cases, bears no resemblance to the needs within the communities themselves. A sustained effort needs to be made to guarantee access to educational opportunities to all Indigenous Australians so that good governance is established within Indigenous communities. New systems need to be developed that incorporate the traditional values and reflect the cultural beliefs within them.

The funding for particularly, incorporated organisations are at the discretion of the grant-giving agency. Applications for funding are made to various agencies under various programs, and it is these agencies that then determine whether the application fits within their guidelines and whether it is of a high enough priority, in comparison with other applications, to be funded. Most Indigenous organisations, even those that have been operating for a decade or more, are dependent on annual grant funding for their continued existence. In practice, most non-profit sector funding agencies force the application of the corporate governance template that is mostly applicable to the profit organisation.

Profit corporate governance principles in non-profit sector

The divergence rather than convergence is manifested in non-profit governance in non-profit boards in Australia. The claim that non-profit manifest features that are alike in appearance to the corporate sector is premature as the non-profit sector is complex and there is much diversity among the types of non-profit organisations and its governance structure. This restricts the view of one-size fits all governance structures.

As a result, two features appear significant. They are the diverse nature of non-profit boards bring efforts to incorporate a representative slice of the organisation's members. Such diversity allows greater involvement of board members and a broader base of skills necessary in board activities such as lobbying for funding. This representation distinguishes non-profit governance structures from the legal or functional specialities evident among corporate sector boards. The second feature identified is the value or ideological foundation.

The non-profit directors and officers generally operate under the same legal standards under state law in terms of managerial obligations and the duties of loyalty and care as their profit peers. However, in contrast to the profit sector, the law plays little role other than inspirational, in assuring accountability in the non-profit sector.

The role of directors of non-profit institutions are more demanding and complex than those of their profit peers, however almost all study evidence suggests that non-profit directors provide less oversight, less effective participation in decision making and in general, less effective governance than their peers in comparable profit corporations. This observation is disturbing especially when non-profit sector receives so much in terms of gifts, grants, tax benefits and other subsidies but is subjected to so few accountability constraints.

In order to overcome this anomaly, it is proposed that profit standards of fiduciary duties be applied to the non-profit sector as it works well. Since both boards are under similar pressures by daily events and activities in the government, business and non-profit, some natural synergies occurs between profit boards and non-profit boards. One of the reasons for this is that board members often overlap these boards.

Profit and non-profit organisations share similar corporate governance practices but the environment in which governance plays out are different. Both boards bear the ultimate responsibility for the organisation and ensuring that it is well managed. This ensures that a well prepared board in the non-profit sector responds to change quickly and thoughtfully and can explore all the possibilities open to it.

Gaps in study

There's been study in the non-profit sector to ascertain if a template for a governance structure from the profit sector would fit into any non-profit sector organisations.

The outcome of these studies has been that one size does not fit all organisations and that every non-profit sector organisation is unique. Each non-profit sector organisation has to customise the governance structure to its particular circumstances.

The gaps in study in the area of corporate governance in Indigenous organisations in Australia is very well summarised as governance involves the interactions among structures, processes and traditions that determine how power is exercised, how decisions are taken, and how citizens or other stakeholders have their say. Fundamentally it is about power, relationships and accountability: who decides, and how decision-makers are held accountable.

There are literally hundreds of Aboriginal and Torres Strait Islander communities within Australia, all struggling to survive. These communities exist because people want them to. They want to keep their cultures, languages and customs alive. And, after continuously occupying this land for 2000 generations why shouldn't they have pride in being members of the oldest living culture in the world. In fact, all Australians should feel a sense of pride in this, very little effort has been made to equip people with the skills to practice good governance in their communities.

A sustained effort needs to be made to guarantee access to educational opportunities to all Indigenous Australians and negotiations need to commence immediately on how to establish good governance within the communities. New systems need to be developed that incorporate the traditional values and reflect the cultural beliefs within them. The current corporations law pay scant regard to this feature of the community life, if at all. Even local government arrangements lack the right mix of conditions for good governance.

There is no doubt that a gap exists in the study in terms of the applicable corporate governance structures for Aboriginal and Torres Strait Islander incorporated organisations in Australia.

Study problem

At its most basic, the study problem is the broad problem that need to be examined more precisely in the study questions. The study problem aims to prompt and place a boundary around the study without specifying what kind of study is to be done.

The discussion of the corporate governance issues in Aboriginal and Torres Strait Islander incorporated organisations has been an on-going one in Australia. The funding bodies of the Indigenous organisations all want their programs to be delivered within their guidelines, which in many cases, bear no resemblance to the needs of the communities.

A major reason for the failure of many intervention programs in Indigenous organisations is that they do not recognise the validity and effectiveness of existing social and organisational structures. Study on the link between cultural values and managerial approaches in Canada suggests that management practices must be flexible, adaptable, and less ethnocentric. The spiritual core value of Native values is a vision of wholeness, where all things are interconnected and interrelated.

The application of corporate governance concepts in the management of Aboriginal and Torres Strait Islander incorporated organisations in Australia needs to consider the implications of the cultural theory. The element of cultural theory must play a significant role in the formulation of any corporate governance model for Aboriginal and Torres Strait Islander incorporated organisations in Australia.

Study Questions (SQ)

SQ 1.	What impact does the powerful Aboriginal cultural influences have on the corporate governance principles in Indigenous organisations?
SQ 2.	What version of corporate governance principles could be applied to Indigenous organisations?
SQ 3.	a) What type of corporate governance training is important for Indigenous organisations? b) What are the outcomes of the training provided to date? c) What evaluation exists for the training? d) Is there a pre-training assessment? e) Is there a post training assessment? f) Is there ongoing knowledge assessment after training has been provided on a cyclic basis such as every 12 months?

What impact does the powerful Aboriginal cultural influences have on the corporate governance principles in Indigenous organisations?

An increasing number of academic writers emphasise critical importance of the need for cultural theory to be part of any corporate governance structure for Aboriginal and Torres Strait Islander incorporated organisation. For instance, the conceptualisation of culture based on a mainstream structural functionalist perspective fails to examine how culture is embedded and entangled in the exercise of power, resistance, and conflict in a given society.

To many Indigenous peoples, kin positions constitute the basic datum of social identity. For Australian Indigenous peoples the core value is relatedness. It is this relatedness, which produces a society where cooperation is valued over competition and where competition among individuals is discouraged.

However, the cultural theory in corporate governance is consistently ignored by funding agencies and academics that argue that the profit sector corporate governance template should be applicable to the Indigenous organisations.

They take little account of cultural matters such as:
- respect for elders;
- obligation to look after one's family and friends;
- obligation to share money and food;
- management roles for women; and
- recognition of the past injustices done to the Indigenous people of Australia.

In summary, this study question aims to capture the cultural influences in decision-making process and the effect it has on the organisations in terms of its performance targets.

What version of corporate governance principles could be applied to Indigenous organisations?

Aboriginal and Torres Strait Islander incorporated organisations form part of the wider family of the non-profit sector organisations. The claim by some writers that non-profit manifest features that are alike in appearance to the corporate sector is premature as the nonprofit sector is complex and there is much diversity among the types of nonprofit organisations and its governance structure. This restricts the view of one-size fits all governance structures.

Profit and non-profit organisations share similar corporate governance practices but the environment in which governance plays out are different. Yet both boards bear the ultimate responsibility for the organisation and ensuring that it is well managed.

What type of corporate governance training is important for Indigenous organisations?

The main emphasis of training and development might be placed upon the development of technical skills, human skills and or conceptual skills. By definition, a technical skill is the ability to use the procedures, techniques, or tools of a specialised field such as directors. A human skill, on the other hand, is the ability to work with, understand, and motivate other people, either as individuals or as groups. Lastly, a conceptual skill is the mental ability to coordinate and integrate all of the organisations interests and activities.

Training and development has the potential to foster distinct competencies which are internal capabilities that bring people to their jobs that may be expressed in a broad, even infinite, array of on-the job behaviours.

The four competencies for the training and development of director's skills is interpersonal, intellectual, business and technical. In terms of any shortcoming in any of the competencies, directors can always rely on expert outside advice on a needs basis.

Background to the model of corporate governance

In deciding upon a set of corporate governance practices that will maximise the potential for the board to add value to the organisation, numerous factors need to be considered including the cultural theory of management in Indigenous organisations. In particular, the practices adopted will reflect the way the board differentiates between the role of the board and that of management. This differentiation of roles will, in turn, be a function of:
- The boards' perception of corporate governance;
- Whether the board places more emphasis on conformance or performance;
- The approach taken by the board to the relationship between the board, management and stakeholders;
- The values and principles of the board; and
- The regulatory, political, and social environment in which the board operates.

The model being proposed is based on wide literature review and forms the basis of a flexible template for the Aboriginal and Torres Strait Islander incorporated organisations. However, this template will need to be customised to fit into the individual needs of the organisations. The recommended model for the governance framework is not intended to be binding but meant as a reference for customisation to individual Aboriginal and Torres Strait Islander incorporated organisation. The details of the various elements of the model are:

Board skills

Ideally the board should collectively have a mix of skills, knowledge and experience in operational expertise relevant to the operation of the organisation; financial and legal skills. Where this is not possible due to the remoteness or the size of the organisation, the board should make arrangements for ready access to such skills on a need basis.

There should also be a clear identification of the powers, roles, responsibilities, and accountabilities between the board and the CEO. The role of the board should be clearly documented in a Board Charter and the board should select the CEO. The definition of roles and powers will serve as ground rules should conflict arise between the board and the CEO.

Board appointments

Appointment processes should ensure that a wide range of suitable and appropriate people are considered for board appointments. The board should be consulted on the skills and experience it needs when new members are being considered for appointment.

Directors should be subject to regular renomination. All new directors should be provided with a letter of appointment setting out their duties and responsibilities.

Board induction and training

Directors should undertake appropriate induction training on appointment. Continuing education and professional development programs should be made available to directors as necessary. There should be on going evaluation of the directors training and a structured pre and post training assessment process.

Board independence

The board chairperson should be independent of management. Where a board member finds that there is a personal conflict, that member should formally declare the conflict and abstain from voting on the issue giving rise to the conflict. The Board Charter should have clear procedures for dealing with these circumstances. Directors should also be involved in the development of the agenda for board meetings and not just leave it to management and the CEO. The board should also try and meet separately of the CEO periodically.

Board meetings and resources

The board should meet regularly at least every two months. Directors should be given adequate notice of meetings. Agenda items, including availability of discussion material should be provided prior to board meetings to enable informed discussion by directors. Minutes of the meetings should accurately record decisions made by the board.

Directors should have reasonable access to independent consultants for investigation and advice. A reasonable budget should be allocated for such advice and filters such as approval by the board chairperson must be considered otherwise the right may be counter-productive. The costs for supporting the board must be transparent and reported.

Code of conduct

The board should approve a written code of conduct setting out ethical and behavioural expectations for both directors and employees. It is critical that both the board and senior management team demonstrate, through their words and actions, an absolute commitment to that code. Only in this manner can a culture of good governance be established within the organisation.

Strategy setting

The objectives of the organisation need to be clearly documented in a longterm corporate strategy and an annual business plan together with achievable and measurable performance targets and milestones. The board should be responsible for approving or rejecting the budget developed by management to achieve the agreed strategy.

Financial and operational reporting

Appropriate and clearly defined performance measures, financial and nonfinancial should be established which enable the efficiency and effectiveness of the organisation to be assessed. Reporting should be tailored to the particular levels of responsibility so that for example, board members are provided with a high level data for decision purposes and management with sufficient detail for management purposes.

The report must be sufficient to communicate the required information but not so extensive and detailed as to hamper comprehension of the key issues. Where possible and culturally appropriate, information should be provided in tabular form or graphical/pictorial presentation to aid comprehension.

Monitoring the performance of the board

The board should adopt procedures to evaluate collectively the performance of the board and individual directors, where feasible, and this should be done at least annually. This could be done using key performance indicators developed for this purpose.

Committee structure

Committee structure would assist the board to utilise the committee to handle sensitive issues while they devote their time on other important matters to run the board effectively. The board can delegate issues for investigation and recommendations to it by the sub-committee. These structures need to be chartered detailing very clearly the committee's roles and responsibilities. Members of the committees can be drawn from a wide area and could even include members from outside the community area of the organisation.

CHAPTER 4

INDIGENOUS ORGANISATION'S PERSPECTIVE

The chosen data collection method was a survey as it is quick, inexpensive, efficient, and accurate way of accessing information about the population. A survey investigation attempts to describe what is happening and consequently is very suitable for descriptive study. A self administered mailed questionnaire was chosen as the Data Collection Instrument as it offers geographical flexibility, is relatively low cost and respondents can take more time to respond at their convenience.

Population and sample size

The majority of the Aboriginal and Torres Strait Islander organisations incorporate under the *Aboriginal Councils and Associations Act* 1976. However, there are others that have been incorporated under the various State and Territory jurisdictions with some incorporated under the Federal regime such as the *Corporations Act* 2001.

Some of these organisations are currently being funded by Aboriginal Hostels Limited (AHL). In order to cover the *Aboriginal Councils and Associations Act* 1976 and all other incorporation jurisdictions, the study sample included all the Aboriginal and Torres Strait islander incorporated organisations that are being funded by AHL. The total sampled organisations that are being funded by AHL is 49 and covers a widespread geographical area.

Location of the sampled organisations

The 49 organisations together operate 59 hostels on a nationwide basis. An analysis of AHL funded organisations revealed that they represent a mixture of jurisdictions under which they are incorporated and these include the State/Territory *Associations Act*, the *Aboriginal Councils and Associations Act* 1976 and the *Corporations Act* 2001.

Analysis of incorporation jurisdictions of the sampled organisations

Incorporation Jurisdictions	Number	%
State/Territory Act	20	41
Aboriginal Councils and Associations Act	23	47
Corporations Act	6	12
TOTAL	49	100

Ethical considerations

As the study for this book included communications with Indigenous people, all the necessary protocols were observed during the study. All the data collected during the survey was obtained in the strictest confidence. The study followed all the necessary steps to ensure that the study covered the requirements of the Aboriginal and Torres Strait Islander protocols for Libraries, Archives and Information Services and those stipulated under other relevant guidelines as well.

Responses received from the sampled organisations

The sampled organisations represent all three levels of incorporation jurisdictions and covered a widespread geographical area.

Geographical spread of the sample

Location	Number of Organisations
Western Australia	9
Northern Territory	5
Queensland	21
New South Wales	8
Victoria	4
South Australia	2
TOTAL	49

A total of 47 responses were received back from the population. This formed the response rate of 96 % that is considered an excellent response for a mailed questionnaire.

Geographical spread of responses received

Location	Questionnaire Sent	Questionnaire Received	(%)
Western Australia	9	9	100
Northern Territory	5	5	100
Queensland	21	20	96
New South Wales	8	7	88
Victoria	4	4	100
South Australia	2	2	100
TOTAL	49	47	96

Data entry: The questionnaire was designed in such way so that it can be analysed using the Microsoft Excel software. Each response was given a value of '1' and was entered into the excel spreadsheet section by section for each variable in every questionnaire. After the data was entered, it was checked for accuracy by three rounds of visual and hard copy inspections.

Patterns of data for study questions:
What impact does the powerful Aboriginal cultural influences have on the corporate governance principles in Indigenous organisations?

This first study question aimed to ascertain the impact powerful Aboriginal cultural influences have on the corporate governance principles in Indigenous organisations. The section presents the overall findings and presents the data as analysed. There was clear agreement on the following:

a) Information of relevance is often shared among the sampled organisations.
b) There are specific and powerful cultural issues that need to be managed on a day-to-day basis and these relate to issues such as respect for elders and other traditional issues, self-determination, autonomy in decision-making, obligation to share money and food, obligation to look after one's family and friends and kinship matters.

These are all important issues in any governance requirements.
c) There is rarely any consideration of cultural issues in the conditions attached by the funding bodies in their governance requirements. If these funding conditions considered the cultural issues, there would be an increase in the participation rate in activities of the sampled organisations by Indigenous Australians.
d) Regular and appropriate financial reports are being provided to the board of the sampled organisations.

There is a clear agreement from the data analysis that Aboriginal cultural influences do have an impact on the corporate governance requirements in Indigenous organisations and these influences need to be managed properly to enable the effective operation. The data as analysed supports this study question.

What version of corporate governance principles could be applied to Indigenous organisations?

This is related to the second study question that aimed to ascertain the version of corporate governance principles that could be applied to Indigenous organisations. The section presents the overall findings and presents the data as analysed. In terms of the general profile of the sampled organisations, there was a clear indication that the majority of the organisations are:
a) Small in size in terms of the number of board members as majority have 6 to 10.
b) Majority of the organisations have 4 to 6 members as quorum for their meetings.
c) There are sufficient meetings of the board in a given year.
d) The overall recorded apologies for the board members are less than 10 days.
e) The agenda and the board papers are given to the board members in more than 5 days prior to a meeting.

There was also agreement on the following:
a) There are rarely any sub-committee structures in place within the organisations.
b) There are rarely any conflict of interest register maintained and often all the declared conflicts were not recorded in the board minutes.
c) Almost all the organisations maintained minutes of their board meetings.
d) There are often any specific and updated policies in place for the recruitment of board members.
e) There is often no board charter detailing the roles and responsibilities of the directors.
f) The chairperson rarely clears the minutes prior to its release and often plays a role in the setting of the board meeting agenda.
g) The sampled organisations often have a corporate plan in place.
h) The imposed corporate governance requirements by funding bodies haven't always been effective to the sampled organisations.
i) Some of the sub-committee structures such as the audit and steering committee for specific tasks are often considered effective for the sampled organisations.

j) The sampled organisations often produce annual reports.
k) The organisations often do not have mechanisms in place to allow board members to have direct access to professional advice on a need basis.
l) Majority of the CEO's in the sampled organisations are selected and appointed by the board.

There is a clear indication from the data analysis that streamlined corporate governance principles should be applied to the Indigenous organisations. The mainstream corporate governance requirements do not fit in well and should be customised to meet the individual sampled organisation's need. The data as collected and analysed supports the study question.

What type of corporate governance training is important for Indigenous organisations?

This related to the question that aimed to ascertain the type of corporate governance training that is important for Indigenous organisations. The section presents the overall findings and presents the data as analysed. There was a clear agreement on the following:

a) There is often no formal orientation-training program for new and existing directors in the sampled organisations.
b) There is often no current training provided to the board members on their role and responsibilities as a director.
c) Sufficient funds are rarely available in the sampled organisations for the corporate governance training.
d) Services of the voluntary organisations have rarely been accessed by the sampled organisations.
e) The following types of corporate governance training is considered suitable to the Indigenous organisations:
   - Role and responsibilities of directors and the board.
   - Strategic management.
   - Understanding financial statements.
   - Board meetings.
   - Code of conduct.
   - Monitoring the performance of the board.
   - Board skills.
   - Board independence.
f) There are rarely any sub-committee structures in place within the organisations.
g) There are rarely any conflict of interest register maintained and often all the declared conflicts were not recorded in the board minutes.
h) Almost all the organisations maintained minutes of their board meetings.
i) There are often any specific and updated policies in place for the recruitment of board members.
j) There is often no Board Charter detailing the roles and responsibilities of the directors.

k) The chairperson rarely clears the minutes prior to its release and often plays a role in the setting of the board meeting agenda.
l) There is a clear agreement that there have been rarely any outcomes for the training provided to date as training is often delivered in the sampled organisations.
m) There was a clear agreement that there was often no evaluation for the training within the sampled organisations.
n) There was a clear agreement that there have been rarely any pre-assessment of training provided in the sampled organisations.
o) There was a clear agreement that there are rarely any post-training assessments in the sampled organisations.
p) There was a clear agreement that there is rarely any on-going knowledge assessment of directors where training had been delivered in the sampled organisations.

The types of corporate governance training that is important to Indigenous organisations are evident from the data as analysed in relation to this study question and the findings have supported the question.

What it means for the corporate governance model

This section is about the appropriate corporate governance models for Aboriginal and Torres Strait Islander organisations, based on what the sampled Aboriginal and Torres Strait Islander incorporated organisations think.

Board Skills

There is a clear agreement that the board skills training is highly suitable for the sampled organisations. As part of this training, the expertise required to select and appoint the chief executive officers can be developed as well.

Board Appointments

There is a clear agreement that the board's role and responsibilities and the financial statement training are highly suitable for the sampled organisations. There are often any specific and updated policies in place for the recruitment of board members. The organisations often do not have mechanisms in place to allow board members to have direct access to professional advice on a need basis.

Board Induction and Training

There was a clear agreement on the following:
a) There is often no formal orientation training program for new and existing directors in the sampled organisations.
b) Sufficient funds are rarely available in the sampled organisations for the corporate governance training.
c) Services of the voluntary organisations have rarely been accessed by the sampled organisations.

d) The board meeting corporate governance training is considered suitable to the Indigenous organisations.
e) There is often any evaluation of training.
f) There is often any pre-assessment and post-assessment of training delivered to directors.
g) There is rarely any on-going knowledge assessment of the directors.
h) The organisations often do not have mechanisms in place to allow board members to have direct access to professional advice on a need basis.

Board Independence

There is a clear agreement that the board's training on independence skills is highly suitable for the sampled organisations and that there are rarely any conflict of interest register maintained.

Board Meetings and Resources

There is a clear agreement that the board meeting training is highly suitable for the sampled Aboriginal and Torres Strait Islander organisations. The sampled organisations also indicated that they all maintain minutes of the board meeting. The majority of the organisations that responded indicated the chairperson rarely clears the minutes prior to its release to other directors.

Code of Conduct

There is a clear agreement that the code of conduct training is highly suitable for the sampled Aboriginal and Torres Strait Islander organisations. There are rarely any conflict of interest registers maintained and often the declared conflicts were not recorded in the board minutes.

Majority of the organisations that responded indicated that the chairperson rarely clears the minutes prior to its release and often plays a role in the setting of the board meeting agenda. Majority of the respondents indicated that they forward the papers to their board members more than five days prior to the actual board meeting.

Strategy Setting

There is a clear agreement that the strategy setting training is highly suitable for the sampled Aboriginal and Torres Strait Islander organisations. The sampled organisations often have a corporate plan in place and often do not have mechanisms in place to allow board members to have direct access to professional advice on a needs basis.

Financial and Operational Reporting

There is a clear agreement that the financial statement training is highly suitable for the sampled Aboriginal and Torres Strait Islander organisations. There is also agreement that often all the declared conflicts were not recorded in the board minutes.

Monitoring the Performance of the Board

There is a clear agreement that the monitoring the performance of the board training is highly suitable for the sampled Aboriginal and Torres Strait Islander organisations. There is often no Board Charter detailing the roles and responsibilities of the directors.

Committee Structure

Some of the sub-committee structures such as the audit and steering committee for specific tasks are often considered effective for the sampled organisations. The imposed corporate governance requirements by funding bodies haven't always been effective to the sampled organisations. There was also a clear agreement that all the sampled organisations often produced annual reports and provided regular and appropriate financial reports to their boards.

CHAPTER 5

CONCLUSIONS AND RECOMMENDATIONS

The purpose of this study is to investigate the study problem as follows:

How can use of corporate governance principles increase participation and effectiveness in Aboriginal and Torres Strait Islander incorporated organisations? The purpose of this final chapter is to draw conclusions about the three study questions and the corporate governance model, to resolve the study problem and to present the implications for theory, policy and practice.

Conclusions about study questions and the corporate governance model

This section examines the conclusions reached about the three study questions and the corporate governance model.

The Indigenous governance background showed how important it was for the governance structure to accommodate the requirements of the culture and traditions of the Indigenous Australians.

The importance placed on sharing and relatedness in Indigenous enterprises illustrates the difficulty of applying western-based management theories in this context. Kinship obligations add a significant non-economic, relational dimension to the management of Indigenous community enterprises and often contribute to their bankruptcy in Western capitalist terms.

In fact, the strength and the nature of obligatory relationships and the web of sharing within kinship networks are often acknowledged as a key determinant of the success or failure of Indigenous enterprises. Yet funding bodies have consistently ignored this factor. Indigenous organisations and communities have been increasingly submitted to accountability and compliance that are in direct conflict with the core Australian Indigenous values of sharing and relatedness. There also has been study in the non-profit sector to ascertain if a template for a governance structure from the profit sector would fit into any non-profit sector organisations.

The outcome of these studies acknowledges that one size does not fit all organisations and that every non-profit sector organisation is unique. Each non-profit sector organisation has to customise the governance structure to its particular circumstances.

Conclusions about study questions
What impact does the powerful Aboriginal cultural influences have on the corporate governance principles in Indigenous organisations?

An increasing number of academic writers emphasise critical importance of the need for cultural theory to be part of any corporate governance structure for Aboriginal and Torres Strait Islander incorporated organisation. For instance, conceptualisation of culture based on a mainstream structural functionalist perspective fails to examine how culture is embedded and entangled in the exercise of power, resistance, and conflict in a given society. Many Indigenous peoples, kin positions constitute the basic datum of social identity. The cultural theory in corporate governance is consistently ignored by funding agencies and academics that argue that the profit sector corporate governance template should be applicable to the Indigenous organisations.

The first study findings has shown that the sampled Aboriginal and Torres Strait Islander incorporated organisations often share information of relevance with other organisations in their area. The results is of importance as the sharing of information is to avoid situations such as staff members who may have been terminated for misconduct in one organisation but is employed by another in the area due to the lack of information. There can be many reasons for this, but the most common one is due to the rivalry between the various Indigenous organisations that goes back many hundreds of years. This particular outcome is new to the corporate governance literature and it is believed that this work will contribute to the body of knowledge.

The results of the second study are all of importance as they deal with the powerful cultural influences that the sampled organisations have to manage on a day-to-day basis. It was found that respect for elders and other traditional issues, obligation to share money and food, obligation to look after one's family and friends and kinship matters are consistent with the corporate governance literature. The study results relating to cultural issues of self-determination and autonomy in decision-making are new to the corporate governance literature and this work will contribute to the body of knowledge.

The results of the third study found that the various conditions attached to the funding rarely considers cultural issues facing the organisation is consistent with the corporate governance literature. The results of the fourth study found that the sampled organisation's board receive regular and appropriate financial reports and is consistent with corporate governance literature.

Finally, the fifth study found that Indigenous people would participate more in the organisation's activities, if funding bodies considered cultural issues, in any corporate governance requirements. This finding is consistent with the corporate governance literature. In brief, all the findings in relation to the first study question illustrate that the powerful cultural influences does have an impact on the corporate governance principles for the sampled Aboriginal and Torres Strait Islander incorporated organisations. The corporate governance model would take into account the findings of the study question one.

What version of corporate governance principles could be applied to Indigenous organisations?

Aboriginal and Torres Strait Islander incorporated organisations form part of the wider family of the non-profit sector organisations. The claim by some writers that non-profit manifest features that are alike in appearance to the corporate sector is premature as the non-profit sector is complex and there is much diversity among the types of non-profit organisations and its governance structure. This restricts the view of one-size fits all governance structures.

The profit and non-profit organisations share similar corporate governance practices but the environment in which governance practices are different. Both boards bear the ultimate responsibility for the organisation to ensure that it is well managed.

The first study finding has shown that the sampled Aboriginal and Torres Strait Islander incorporated organisations rarely have sub-committee structures in place. The sub-committee structures are considered necessary to assist in the process of greater transparency in the decision making process of the organisations. The study finding is inconsistent with the corporate governance literature and it is believed that this work will contribute to the body of knowledge.

The second and fourth study found that the sampled organisations rarely maintain a conflict of interest register and often all declared conflicts of interest is not recorded in the minutes of the board meetings are of importance. Maintaining the conflict of interest register and recording the declared conflicts in the board minutes are considered to be best practice in the corporate governance literature. However, the results from this study need to be considered in the context of the cultural issues and in particular the kinship issues where Indigenous people are under social obligation to share money and food and to look after one's family and friends.

This obligation forces them to employ their family and friends in the community organisations resulting in the need to maintain the conflict of interest register and recording of the conflict in the minutes as irrelevant. The need for the register and recording of conflicts in the board minutes may be relevant in the urban organisations but those in the rural and remote areas (where the social structures and traditional beliefs are very strong), the need is irrelevant. These finding go against the western theories of corporate governance and is therefore inconsistent with the corporate governance literature. This finding is believed to be of value to the body of knowledge.

The third study finding that minutes of the board meetings are being maintained in the sampled organisations is consistent with the corporate governance literature.

The fifth study found that the chairperson rarely clears the minutes of the board meetings before they are released is against the recommended best practice of corporate governance principles. The study found that the board agenda is often set in consultation with the chairperson is also linked to the fifth finding. One of the reasons for this could be due to the literacy skills of the chairperson. The findings are inconsistent with the corporate governance literature and this work is expected to contribute to the body of knowledge.

The study results of six and seven found that there are often no specific policies in place for the recruitment of board members and that there is often no board charters in place in the sampled organisations are against the best practice guide of corporate governance principles. All non-profit organisations must formulate a clear statement of individual board member responsibilities adapted to the organisation's needs and circumstances to assist with the process of recruiting new board members by clarifying expectations before candidates accept nomination. The findings are inconsistent with the corporate governance literature and this work is expected to contribute to the body of knowledge.

The eighth study found that corporate plans are often maintained in the sampled organisations as against the best practice guide of corporate governance principles. The finding is inconsistent with the corporate governance literature and this work is expected to contribute to the body of knowledge.

The ninth study found that the audit committee and steering committee for specific tasks would assist in the greater transparency in the decision making process are consistent with the corporate governance literature.

The study finding of a need for the cultural issues committee to assist in the operation of the sampled organisations and to enhance their transparency in the decision making process is new to the corporate governance literature. The cultural issues committee will be responsible to consider cultural issues such as the kinship matters and the social obligation issues of members to ensure everything is kept above board. This work is expected to contribute to the body of knowledge.

The tenth study found that the sampled organisations often produce annual reports is against the best practice guide of corporate governance principles. The finding is inconsistent with the corporate governance literature and this work is expected to contribute to the body of knowledge.

The eleventh study found that the board selects and appoints the CEO of the organisations and this is consistent with the corporate governance literature.

Finally, the twelfth study found that the board of the sampled organisations often do not have access to professional advice on a need basis is inconsistent with the best practice guide in the corporate governance literature. The main reason for this shortcoming is due to the location of the sampled organisations, the availability of the professionals and the cost factor as well. This work is expected to contribute to the body of knowledge.

In summary, all the findings in relation to second study question illustrate that the streamlined corporate governance principles should be applied to the Indigenous organisations. The mainstream corporate governance requirements do not fit in well and should be customised to meet the individual sampled organisation's need.

What type of corporate governance training is important for Indigenous organisations?

Training and development has the potential to foster distinct competencies which are internal capabilities that bring people to their jobs that may be expressed in a broad, even infinite, array of on-the-job behaviours.

The first and second study results have shown that the sampled Aboriginal and Torres Strait Islander incorporated organisations often do not have any formal orientation program in place for the new and existing directors. The orientation program is considered necessary to assist in the understanding of the organisation and the role and responsibilities of the directors. The study findings are new to the corporate governance literature and it is believed to be of value to the body of knowledge.

The third study found that the sampled organisations rarely have sufficient funds for corporate governance training is new to the corporate governance literature. Majority of the sampled organisations depend solely on the funds from the funding bodies that do not cater for training but are solely focused on the program delivery. Majority of such programs fail due to this oversight and lack of consideration for the cultural issues in Indigenous organisations. It is believed to be of value to the body of knowledge.

The fourth study found that the services of the volunteers to deliver corporate governance training have rarely been accessed. The study finding is new to the corporate governance literature and it is believed to be of value to the body of knowledge.

The fifth study revealed that the types of corporate governance training suitable for Indigenous organisations are role and responsibilities of directors and the board, strategic management, understanding financial statements, board meetings, code of conduct, monitoring the performance of the board, board skills and board independence. This finding is consistent with the corporate governance literature.

The results of the sixth and seventh study found that there have been rarely any outcomes for the training provided to date and there is also often no evaluation of training to directors. The study findings are new to the corporate governance literature and it is believed to be of value to the body of knowledge.

The eighth and ninth study results deal with training pre-assessment, post-assessment, and ongoing knowledge assessment. The study found that there are rarely any pre-assessment prior to training being delivered, rarely any post-assessment after the training had been delivered and rarely any on-going knowledge assessment to ascertain the need for further training. The study findings are new to the corporate governance literature and it is believed to be of value to the body of knowledge.

Conclusions about the corporate governance model

The model is based on the corporate governance literature and will form the basis of a template for the Aboriginal and Torres Strait Islander incorporated organisations in Australia.

The recommended model for the governance framework is not intended to be binding but meant to serve as a reference for customisation to individual Aboriginal and Torres Strait Islander incorporated organisation.

Corporate governance model: study findings

The results of the first study has shown that the sampled Aboriginal and Torres Strait Islander incorporated organisations agreed that the board skills is an important area of a model and that training in this area is highly desirable. The finding is consistent with the corporate governance literature.

The second study found that there are often no policies in place for the recruitment of board members as well as rarely any access to professional advice on a need basis is inconsistent with the corporate governance literature. This work is expected to contribute to the body of knowledge.

The third study found that there are often no board induction and training in the sampled organisations is inconsistent with the corporate governance literature. This work is expected to contribute to the body of knowledge.

The fourth study found that the board independence type training is highly desirable is consistent with the literature. However, the finding that there are rarely any conflicts of interest registers maintained is inconsistent with the corporate governance literature. This work is expected to contribute to the body of knowledge.

The fifth study found that the board meeting and resources type training is highly desirable is consistent with the corporate governance literature.

The sixth and seventh study results found that the code of conduct and strategy setting type training are highly desirable and are consistent with the corporate governance literature.

The results from the eighth and ninth study found that the financial and operating reporting and the monitoring of the performance of the board type training are highly desirable are consistent with the corporate governance literature.

Finally, the tenth study found that some of the sub-committee structures are suitable to the sampled organisations is new to the corporate governance literature. The committees that would add value to the Indigenous organisations are audit committees, steering committees for specific tasks and the cultural issues committees. The remuneration and appointments committee (for staff and directors) and the corporate governance committees were considered as irrelevant. As the study finding is new to the corporate governance literature, it is believed that this work will contribute to the body of knowledge.

How can use of corporate governance principles increase participation and effectiveness in Aboriginal and Torres Strait Islander incorporated organisations?

In order to answer this question, first a study problem and three study questions were defined and a corporate governance model developed in an attempt to shed light on increased participation and effectiveness in Indigenous organisations in Australia.

The sub-committee structure in the model will need to be customised for individual organisation's requirements. The study findings have shown that all types of sub-committee structure are not suitable for the sampled organisations.

Access to professional advisers on a need basis was also a major problem within the sampled organisations. As limited resources are available to Aboriginal and Torres Strait Islander incorporated organisations, it is not always feasible to get professional advisers and consultants.

Two checklists have been developed after considering all the study findings that can be used by Aboriginal and Torres Strait Islander incorporated organisations to assess the adequacy of their corporate governance.

The first checklist is designed mainly for the urban and suburban organisations (where the social structures and traditional beliefs are not very strong) to assess the strengths and weaknesses of their current governance framework. Those items that are excluded in the second checklist are highlighted in bold.

Corporate governance checklist for urban and sub-urban Indigenous Organisations

Board Appointments and Training:	1. Are new board members appropriately inducted on appointment regarding the organisation and their responsibilities? 2. Is the basis for board appointments clearly stated? 3. Is there pre and post assessment of any training provided? 4. Is there on-going knowledge assessment of directors for training purposes? 5. Is there any training needs analysis process in place for all directors? 6. Is there sufficient training budget and adequate process in place to seek assistance from Agencies set up to provide free training to Indigenous organisations?
Definition of Roles and Powers:	1. Are the roles of the board and the CEO clearly defined? 2. Is the role of the board documented in a Board Charter? 3. Is there a clearly defined division of responsibilities within the organisation?
Board Skills, Independence and Resources:	1. Is the board chair independent of management? 2. Is there sufficient mix of financial and operational skills within the board to ensure it can effectively direct and monitor the organisation's activities? 3. Are there appropriate arrangements to ensure that the board has access to all relevant information and professional advise on a need basis to enable it to carry out its functions efficiently and effectively? 4. **Are there procedures in place to address the issues of conflict of interest?**
Code of Conduct:	1. Has the board developed a formal code of conduct defining the standards of personal behaviour to which members of the board and all employees of the organisation are required to adhere? 2. Do the board and senior management lead by example in relation to the code of conduct?
Strategy Setting:	1. Are the long-term objectives clearly stated in the corporate plan and approved by the board? 2. Is the annual budget prepared by management and approved by the board?
Financial and Operational Reporting:	1. Are the reports to the board include financial, non-financial, and appropriate information to facilitate a comprehensive review? 2. Are the users of the report (specially the board members) satisfied with the amount and quality of the information provided? 3. Are the reports provided to the board on a regular basis?
Sub-committees:	1. Are sufficient members on the sub-committees who are independent of management? 2. **Does the committee have a written charter setting out its role and responsibilities?** 3. Does the committee have sufficient resources to discharge its responsibilities effectively including professional advice where required?

The second checklist is designed mainly for the rural and remote based organisations (where the social structures and traditional beliefs are very strong) to assess the strengths and weaknesses of their current governance framework. This checklist was designed in the context of the cultural issues and in particular the kinship issues where Indigenous people are under social obligation to share money and food and to look after one's family and friends.

Corporate governance checklist for rural and remote indigenous organisations

Board Appointments and Training:	1. Are new board members appropriately inducted on appointment regarding the organisation and their responsibilities? 2. Is there pre and post assessment of any training provided? 3. Is there on-going knowledge assessment of directors for training purposes? 4. Is there any training needs analysis process in place for all directors? 5. Is there sufficient training budget and adequate process in place to seek assistance from Agencies set up to provide free training to Indigenous organisations?
Definition of Roles and Powers:	1. Are the roles of the board and the CEO clearly defined? 2. Is the role of the board documented in a Board Charter? 3. Is there a clearly defined division of responsibilities within the organisation?
Board Skills, Independence and Resources:	1. Is the board chair independent of management? 2. Is there sufficient mix of financial and operational skills within the board to ensure it can effectively direct and monitor the organisation's activities? 3. Are there appropriate arrangements to ensure that the board has access to all relevant information and professional advise on a need basis to enable it to carry out its functions efficiently and effectively?
Code of Conduct:	1. Has the board developed a formal code of conduct defining the standards of personal behaviour to which members of the board and all employees of the organisation are required to adhere? 2. Do the board and senior management lead by example in relation to the code of conduct?
Strategy Setting:	1. Are the long-term objectives clearly stated in the corporate plan and approved by the board? 2. Is the annual budget prepared by management and approved by the board?
Financial and Operational Reporting:	1. Are the reports to the board include financial, non-financial, and appropriate information to facilitate a comprehensive review? 2. Are the users of the report (specially the board members) satisfied with the amount and quality of the information provided? 3. Are the reports provided to the board on a regular basis?
Sub-committees:	1. Are sufficient members on the sub-committees who are independent of management? 2. Does the committee have sufficient resources to discharge its responsibilities effectively including professional advice where required?

Implications for theory

The conceptualisation of culture based on a mainstream structural functionalist perspective fails to examine how culture is embedded and entangled in the exercise of power, resistance, and conflict in a given society. For many Indigenous peoples, kin positions constitute the basic datum of social identity. Kinship rules prescribe 'what must be done', and also 'what must not be done' in relation to matters of marriage, food gathering, sharing of food and other goods, trading among communities and educational roles. The analysis of data provided a richer understanding of the issues affecting Aboriginal and Torres Strait Islander incorporated organisations in Australia in terms of the current practices of corporate governance. Thus, this study confirms the usefulness of the survey questionnaire methodology.

Implications for policy and practice

A survey of the literature on corporate governance discovered that an increasing number of academic writers emphasise critical importance of the need for cultural theory to be part of any corporate governance structure for Aboriginal and Torres Strait Islander incorporated organisation. The cultural theory in corporate governance is consistently ignored by funding agencies and academics that argue that the profit sector corporate governance template should be applicable to the Indigenous organisations.

A major reason for the failure of many intervention programs in Indigenous organisations is that they do not recognise the validity and effectiveness of existing social and organisational structures. Study on the link between cultural values and managerial approaches in Canada suggests that management practices must be flexible, adaptable, and less ethnocentric. The spiritual core value is a vision of wholeness, where all things are interconnected and interrelated.

This study has eventuated in the revised elements of corporate governance and two corporate governance checklists. The two checklists are designed to assess the adequacy of the corporate governance within the Aboriginal and Torres Strait Islander incorporated organisations.

Limitations

This study examined the scope for the application of corporate governance concepts in the management of Aboriginal and Torres Strait Islander incorporated organisations in Australia. The survey questionnaire was limited to the 49 organisations being funded under AHL's Community Hostel Grants program. The findings arising out of the study are confined to the sampled organisations and may not apply to the entire Aboriginal and Torres Strait Islander incorporated organisations in Australia. Therefore, they may not be generalised across Australia or even across countries. Further study will need to be conducted in other Indigenous organisations and countries to confirm these findings.

Further study

This study examined the scope for the application of corporate governance concepts in the management of Aboriginal and Torres Strait Islander incorporated organisations in Australia. The conclusions and recommendations provide a foundation for further study. In order to obtain a deeper understanding of the issues involved, it will be imperative to conduct further study into one or all of the following three areas:
- Extend the study,

- Adopt the methodology but qualify the results,
- Focus upon the role of the various incorporation jurisdictions for Indigenous people and consider duplication of services.

Firstly, there is an opportunity to replicate the study in other environments. This will help determine how robust the findings are and how easily findings may be transported. This could be approached in several ways. This study was confined to the organisations funded by AHL under its Community Hostels Grant program. To test the results, a study needs to be conducted on a much wider scale with a large sample of Aboriginal and Torres Strait Islander organisations in Australia.

Such a study needs to be conducted both on qualitative and quantitative methodologies and can also be conducted in other countries that have better and more matured corporate governance structures and practices for its Indigenous people such as Canada and the United States of America, as well as the Pacific Island countries such as Fiji Islands, Vanuatu and Papua New Guinea, where corporate governance practices are in developing stages.

Secondly, the findings of this study relied upon quantitative methodology by utilising the descriptive survey questionnaire. These findings will be given further credibility by conducting a qualitative study, involving case study and in-depth interviewing.

Lastly, this study covered a spectrum of incorporation jurisdictions available to Aboriginal and Torres Strait Islander people in Australia to incorporate their organisation. This ranges from the jurisdictions in the State/Territory to the Federal arena. There is also a specific legislation set up in 1976 *Aboriginal Council and Associations Act* 1976 for Indigenous Australians to incorporate under and avoid complexities involved with other jurisdictions. While most Indigenous organisations have incorporated under this legislation, there are also substantial numbers that prefer other jurisdictions resulting in duplication of services to Indigenous Australians. There is a potential for further study in this area to find out the success or failure of the *Aboriginal Council and Associations Act* 1976.

Overall, there are several avenues through which further study may be pursued. The most constructive way may be by replicating this study in other environments to ascertain how applicable the findings are. A sample of study propositions for these sorts of study could be:

1. What are the relationships between corporate governance structures for Indigenous organisations in comparison with the commercial environments in Australia?
2. What are the requirements for the cultural issues to be incorporated into any corporate governance training for Indigenous organisations?
3. What are the relationships between the requirements of the corporate governance and its usefulness between the various incorporation legislations available to Indigenous Australians?

Final remarks

Corporate governance concepts in the Aboriginal and Torres Strait Islander incorporated organisations have been mainly built around the western theories with no major study done in the area to ascertain its suitability in the cultural context. There has been study done in the non-profit sector to ascertain if a template for a governance structure from the profit sector would fit into any non-profit sector organisations, the outcome of which has been that one size does not fit all and that every non-profit sector organisation is unique. Each non-profit sector organisation has to customise the governance structure to its particular circumstances.

The objective of this study was to explicitly illustrate that the use of corporate governance principles would increase participation and effectiveness in Aboriginal and Torres Strait Islander incorporated organisations. The study adopted the descriptive survey mail questionnaire as the main methodology.

The study selected all Aboriginal and Torres Strait Islander incorporated organisations that are funded by AHL under its Community Hostels Grant program. This included 49 organisations across Australia. A total of 47 responses were received representing a response rate of 96%.

Upon data collection and data analysis, the following major findings emerged. Firstly, the various conditions attached by funding bodies rarely consider cultural issues facing the Indigenous organisations. Indigenous people would participate more in the organisation's activities if the funding organisations consider cultural issues in any corporate governance requirements. Secondly, the sampled organisations often do not have access to professional advice on a needs basis.

Thirdly, there was rarely any evaluation of training, pre-assessment of training, post-assessment of training and on-going knowledge assessment of directors to maintain currency of the knowledge and expertise required in fulfilling the role and responsibilities of a director.

Fourthly, there was a clear indication for the need of a separate corporate governance checklist for the urban and suburban Indigenous organisations where the social structures and traditional beliefs are not very strong and a separate checklist for rural and remote area where the social structures and traditional beliefs are very strong.

Consequently, it has been concluded, that:
(1) Funding organisations must consider cultural issues facing Indigenous organisations to ensure the success of its programs, that
(2) Indigenous organisations must ensure that they have access to professional advice on a needs basis and
(3) All training activities be conducted properly with proper evaluation of training, pre-assessment prior to delivery, post-assessment after delivery and on-going knowledge assessment.

Finally, the conclusions and recommendations provide a solid foundation for further study. This will be imperative in order to obtain a deeper understanding of the issues involved.

BIBLIOGRAPHY

Adams, H. 1989, 'Prison of grass', Saskatoon, SK: Fifth House.

Adams, M. A. 2002, 'The convergence of international corporate systems – where is Australia heading? (Part 1)', *Keeping Good Companies Journal*, February, vol.54, no. 1.

Adams, M. A. 2002, 'The convergence of international corporate systems – where is Australia heading? (Part 2)', *Keeping Good Companies Journal*, March, vol.54, no. 2.

Adler, N.J. 1991, International dimensions of organisational behaviour (2nd ed.), Boston.

Anders, G.C. & Anders, K.K. 1986, 'Incompatible goals in unconventional organisations: The politics of Alaska Native Corporations'. Organisational Studies, vol. 7.

Bains, N. & Band, D. 1996, *'Winning Ways through Corporate Governance'* Kent: Mackays of Catham.

Barratt, P. 1995, *'Corporate governance and the role of Australia 2010'*, Business Council Bulletin, July.

Barratt, P. 1999, *'Corporate governance in Commonwealth Authorities and Companies'*, Principles and Better Practices, Discussion Paper, Australian National Audit Office, Canberra.

Bartlett, B. 1999, 'Health services development: New Doctor', *Journal of the Doctors Reform Society*, Summer 1998/1999, vol. 6.

Beckett, J.R. 1988, *Past and Present: The Construction of Aboriginality*, Aboriginal Studies Press, Canberra.

Bennett, S. 1989, *Aborigines and Political Power*, Allen and Unwin, Sydney.

Berndt, R.M. & Tonkinson, R. 1988, *Social Anthropology and Australian Aboriginal Studies: A Contemporary Overview*, Aboriginal Studies Press, Canberra.

Blair, M.M. 1994, *Ownership and Control, rethinking Corporate Governance for the Twenty First Century*, Brooking Inst.

Blair, M.M. 1995, *Ownership and Control*, the Brookings Institutions, Washington, D.C.

Blunt, P. & Warren, D.M. 1996, Indigenous organisations, and development. London: Intermediate Technology Publications.

Bosch, H. 1995, Corporate Practices and Conduct, 3rd Ed.

Chase, A. & Sutton, P. 1987, 'Australian Aborigines in a rich environment', in Edwards, W.H. (Ed.), Traditional Aboriginal Society. A Reader, Macmillan, South Melbourne.

Cohen, P. & Somerville, M. 1990, Ingelba and the Five Black Matriarchs, Allen & Unwin, Australia, Sydney.

Coombs, H.C. 1994, *Aboriginal Autonomy, issues and strategies*, Cambridge University Press, Cambridge, United Kingdom.

Crawford, F. 1989, Jalinardi Ways: Whitefellas Working in Aboriginal Community, Curtin University of Technology, Perth.

Dacks, G. 1983, Worker-controlled Native enterprises: A vehicle for community development in Northern Canada? The Canadian Journal of Native Studies, vol. 3, pp. 289-310.

Davis, J.H., Schoorman, E.D., & Donaldson, L. 1997, ' Toward a Stewardship Theory of Management', Academy of Management Review, vol. 22, no. 1.

Demb, A. & Neubauer, F. 1992, *The Corporate Board: Confronting the Paradoxes*.

Dobson, J. 1991, 'Ethics of Shareholder Referendums: Corporate Democracy or Hypocrispy?', Review of Business, vol. 13, no. 3.

Donaldson, L. & Davis, J. H. 1994, 'Boards and Company Performance – Research challenges the conventional Wisdom', *Corporate Governance: An International Review*, vol. 2, no.3.

Dumont, J. 1993, Justice and aboriginal people. In Aboriginal peoples and the justice system: Report of the National Roundtable on Aboriginal Justice Issues by the Royal Commission on Aboriginal Peoples. Ottawa, ON: Canada Communication group Publishing.

Eades, D. 1998, 'They don't speak an Aboriginal Language, or do they?' in Keen, I. (Ed.), Being Black: Aboriginal Cultures in 'Settled' Australia, Aboriginal Studies Press, Canberra.

Eisenhardt, K.M. 1989, 'Agency theory: an assessment and review', *Academy of Management Review*, vol. 14, no. 1.

Fama, E. & Jensen, M. 1983a, 'Agency problems and Residual Claims', *Journal of Law and Economics*, vol. 26.

Frideres, J.S. 1993, Native peoples in Canada: Contemporary conflicts (4th ed.). Scarborough, ON: Prentice Hall.

Gill, M. 2001, 'Governance DO'S & DON'T'S: Lessons from Case Studies on twenty Canadian Non-profits, Final Report' *The Institute On Governance*, Canada.

Greer, S. & Patel, C. 2000, 'The issue of Australian indigenous world-views and accounting', *Accounting, Auditing & Accountability Journal*, Bradford 2000.

Harrison, J.S. & Fiet, J.O. 1999, 'New CEO's pursue their own self-interests by sacrificing stakeholder value', *Journal of Business Ethics*, April, vol. 19, no. 3.

Harris, S. 1990, *Two-way Aboriginal Schooling*, Aboriginal Studies Press, Canberra, ACT.

Herbet, P., MacMillan, K. & Dulewicz, V. 1995, 'The development of standards of good practice for boards of directors', *Executive Development*, Bradford vol. 8, no. 6.

Hiatt, L.R. 1986, *Aboriginal Political Life: The Wentworth Lecture 1984*, Australian Institute of Aboriginal and Torres Strait Islander Studies, Canberra.

Hofstede, G. 1993, 'Cultures and organisations: Software of the mind'. London: McGraw Hill.

Ingram, R.T. 1998, '*Ten Basic Responsibilities of Non-profit Boards*', National Center for Non-profit Boards, Washington, DC, USA.

Jensen, M.C. & Meckling, W.H. 1976, 'Theory of the Firm: Managerial Behaviour, Agency Costs and Ownership Structure', *Journal of Financial Economics*, vol. 3.

Keeffe, K. 1992, From Centre to the City: *Aboriginal Education, Culture and Power*, Aboriginal Studies Press, Canberra.

Kellehear, A. 1993, '*The Unobstrusive Researcher*', Allen & Unwin, Sydney.

Lawlor, R. 1991, 'Voices of the First Day: Awakening in the Australian Dreamtime', Inner Traditions International Ltd, Rochester, VT.

Lincoln, Y.S., and Guba, E.G. 1985, *Naturalistic Inquiry*. Newbury Park, Calif.: Sage.

Lyons, M. 1991, 'Non-profit Organisations in Australia: What Do We Know and What Should We Find Out Next?' Working Paper No. 1, Program on Non-profit Corporations, Queensland University of Technology.

Lyons, M. 2001, '*Third Sector: the contribution of non-profit and cooperative enterprises in Australia*'. Allen & Unwin, Crows Nest, NSW.

Maybury-Lewis, D. 1992, 'Millennium: Tribal Wisdom and the Modern World', penguin Books, New York, NY.

McCorquodale, J. 1987, *Aborigines and the Law*: A Digest, Aboriginal Studies Press, Canberra.

Meggitt, M.J. 1962, *Desert People: A Study of the Walbiri Aborigines of Central Australia*, Angus and Robertson, Sydney.

Monks, R.A.G. & Minow, N. 1989,	'The High Cost of Ethical Retrigression', *Directors and Boards,* vol. 13.
Monks, R.A.G. & Minow, N. 1996,	*Watching the Watchers*, Blackwell, Cambridge, MA.
Pfeffer, J. 1972,	'Size and composition of corporate boards of directors: the organisations and its environment', *Administrative Science Quarterly*, vol.17.
Redpath, L. 1997,	'A comparison of native culture, non-native culture and new management ideology', Administrative Sciences Association of Canada, September.
Sansom, B. 1988,	'A grammar of exchange', in Keen, I. (Ed), Being Black: Aboriginal Cultures in 'Settled' Australia, Australian Institute of Aboriginal Studies, Canberra.
Scheffler, H.W. 1978,	*Australian Kin Classification*, Cambridge Studies in Anthropology 23, CUP, London.
Steane, P. & Christie, M. 2001,	'Non-profit boards in Australia: a distinctive governance approach', *Corporate Governance: An International Review,* vol. 9, no. 1.
Swain, T. 1993,	'A Place for Strangers: Towards a History of Australian Aboriginal Being', Cambridge University Press, Cambridge.
Tricker, R.I. 2000,	'*Corporate Governance*', Dartmouth Publishing Company, Aldershot, England.
Toyne, P. & Vachon, D. 1984,	'Growing up the Country: The Pitjantjatjara Struggle for their Land', McPhee Gribble Publishers, Victoria.
Turner, P. 2001,	'Reconciliation – Moving beyond broad support and goodwill', Paper presented to the 15th Lionel Murphy Memorial Lecture, NSW Parliament House, 28 September.
Twaits, A. 1998,	'The duties of Officers and Employees in Non-profit Organisations' *Bond Law Review,* vol. 10.
Williams, N.M. 1986,	'The Yolngu and Their Land: A System of Land Tenure and the Fight for its Recognition', Australian Institute of Aboriginal Studies, Canberra.
Young, E. 1987,	'Commerce in the bush: Aboriginal and Inuit experiences in the commercial world', Australian Aboriginal Studies, No. 2.

AUTHOR'S PROFILE

Dr Kamlesh Sharma
BA, MBA, MCom, Grad Dip CSP, DBA, JP, ASA, FCIS, FPNA, FAICD.

Dr Sharma lives in Canberra and is the Assistant General Manager and Company Secretary of Aboriginal Hostels Limited (a company wholly owned by the Australian Government). Prior to this, he worked in financial and administrative roles with South Pacific Applied Geoscience Commission, Shell Fiji Limited, ANZ Banking Group Limited and the Office of the Auditor General in Fiji.

Born in Korovuto, Nadi, Fiji Islands, Dr Sharma finished his primary education at Korovuto Primary School and secondary education at Korovuto Secondary and Sangam College in Nadi. Dr Sharma has Bachelor of Arts Degree in Accounting and Economics from the University of the South Pacific in Suva, Fiji Islands, Master of Business Administration with majors in Human Resources, Local Government, Public Sector and Association Management, Master of Commerce with majors in Accounting, Finance and Entrepreneurship from the University of New England, Armidale, NSW, Graduate Diploma in Company Secretarial Practice from Chartered Secretaries Australia and Doctor of Business Administration from Southern Cross University in Lismore, NSW.

Dr Sharma is a Justice of the Peace Officer in Australian Capital Territory, an associate member of Certified Practising Accountants (CPA) Australia, Fellow of the Institute of Chartered Secretaries Australia, Fellow Professional National Accountant of the National Institute of Accountants and Fellow of the Australian Institute of Company Directors.

COMMENDATIONS

Traditional structures for Indigenous Australians have provided the basis for governance and survival over thousands of years. Over a number of years I have witnessed a trend to ignore or separate out the core traditional values and the roles of traditional stakeholders in the setting of governance structures for Aboriginal organisations. In the time of significant change from 'superintendent's and Government's managing the lives of our people' to the new era of self management and self determination there was a view, in parts of the country I am familiar with, that organisational structures were not the domain of the elders and their values but rather management groups had to focus on accountability to fund providers.

We are currently moving to a new era of change, which will not be successful if it doesn't incorporate the goals, aspirations, and priorities of the local traditional arrangements.

The most successful Aboriginal organisations that I am familiar with have a blend of textbook corporate arrangements and the involvement of the elders, who understand the need for strong corporate governance, but they also ensure that the wellbeing of the people is understood.

As an Aboriginal person who has spent the past 29 years in management at the community, regional and national level, I welcome the work and findings of Dr Sharma. It is my hope that this work, which is just plain common sense, inspires Aboriginal managers and their advisers to look at the issues and ensure that the values we hold so strongly are manifested in the ways we participate in our governance structures.

Ron Morony PSM
General Manager, Indigenous Business Australia, Canberra.

====

Corporate governance can be dated back to the Swiss cantons of the 1300s, but Indigenous governance can be traced back many 1000s of years. There are many excellent books on the topic of both private and public sector governance, but there is little detailed examination of the subject of Indigenous governance. This book, based upon the research and doctoral studies of Dr Kamlesh Sharma, who works within the Aboriginal Hostels Limited (AHL) environment, is a valuable asset to the literature.

As someone who specialises in corporate law and corporate governance, I knew little of Indigenous governance until I read Dr Sharma thesis as one of his external examiners. I had previously been a lecturer of Kamlesh in corporate law and I had worked with AHL in the area of governance and was impressed by his in-depth knowledge of this complex area. This book is a dedication to hardwork, clear thinking, expanding the knowledge base of all involved in governance and in particular the specific issues that arise with Indigenous organisations.

Professor Michael A Adams
Professor of Corporate Law, , Faculty of Law, University of Technology, Sydney.

====

Corporate governance is concerned with the process by which corporate bodies are subjected to accountability mechanisms. It is concerned with the manner in which the organisation is made accountable to and transparent in its dealings with all stakeholders and focuses on the way in which the board ensures that an organisation is accountable to its members and stakeholders. Irrespective of the systems and procedures in place, to ensure proper governance processes, the culture of an organisation and that of its leaders will determine whether governance processes will be effective.

The book addresses these issues, including the varying needs of members, and provides practical and constructive solutions to identified problems. The research, its findings and suggested solutions provides a solid foundation for further study and is recommended reading.

Dr. Sharma is to be commended for the professional manner in which he has conducted this research.

Paul Moni
National President, Chartered Secretaries Australia, Sydney.

====

The findings of this book present a powerful argument for greater regard to be given to cultural factors when governments and other organisations attempt to assist the Indigenous community. It is a credit to Dr Sharma that he has produced such a compelling publication on corporate governance within the Indigenous community at a time when the community at large has concerned itself with governance of listed companies and public sector organisations. I hope the lessons in this work are heeded by all individuals and organisations that have any involvement with Indigenous Australians. The National Institute of Accountants congratulates Dr Sharma on the quality and content of this publication.

Roger Cotton
Chief Executive Officer, National Institute of Accountants, Melbourne.

====

Through comprehensive and diligent research Dr Sharma has produced an exceptional publication entitled 'Indigenous Governance'. This book I have no doubt will prove to be a beacon in the night illuminating those very important areas of corporate governance that clearly need defining for both Indigenous and non-Indigenous Australians.

Through his selfless dedication to study and his unremitting efforts in articulating the importance of corporate governance in how it impacts not only on government agencies at all levels but also how it creates a binding and strong nexus with the private sector.

Dr Sharma's masterly crafted document presents in itself a valuable resource, theoretically speaking, for all scholars and academics alike who are pursuing studies in business administration, it also very importantly makes for a blueprint and compass for those peoples who are engaged in commerce generally.

I feel privileged to have been asked to provide comment in relation to Dr Sharma's most informative and elucidating publication on Indigenous governance and I commend him on his fine efforts and most generous sharing of his wealth of knowledge and intellect on such an important topic.

Dr Colin W Dillon APM
Special Indigenous Advisor, Department of Aboriginal and Torres Strait Islander Policy, Brisbane.

====

Kamlesh in his research focussed on two key research issues: namely, the scope for the application of corporate governance concepts in the management of Indigenous incorporated bodies and the means of improving Indigenous participation and the effectiveness of those bodies. Contrary to the common belief that the corporate governance concept is foreign to many Indigenous people, Kamlesh demonstrates from his analysis that corporate governance principles could enhance Indigenous participation as well as the effectiveness of Indigenous incorporated organisations. To increase the participation and effectiveness of these organisations, Kamlesh proposes that the cultural element be incorporated in the governance structures of these organisations. Furthermore, Kamlesh in his research rightly points out a key gap in contemporary corporate governance in incorporated organisations: the lack of an on-going evaluations program and proper training to improve the corporate knowledge, skills and expertise of the corporate directors. Although the focus of the research only covers incorporated organisations funded by Aboriginal Hostels Ltd its findings has wide application to corporate governance issues in other sectors as well as providing a sound foundation for further research in this area.

Rodney Alfredson
Director, Office of Evaluation and Audit, Department of Finance and Administration, Canberra.

====

Kamlesh is to be congratulated for his analysis of corporate governance in Indigenous organisations and his contribution to our understanding of a subject which impacts on both public policy and reconciliation. As he points out in his book, this is an area of business practice, which is little understood and where few have attempted scholarship.

His survey of a significant sample of organisations providing valuable and, indeed, essential services to Australia's indigenous people has enhanced our understanding of the governance practices of these organisations. Kamlesh's check lists will provide a useful basis for Indigenous organisations to examine their practices and he has flagged areas in which further research would benefit our understanding of the interaction of indigenous culture and the prevailing legal and administrative systems.

Alan Doolan
Executive Director, Adept Associates Pty Limited, Canberra.